STRENGTH FROM SHADOWS

STRENGTH
FROM
SHADOWS

R. Earl Allen

BROADMAN PRESS

Nashville, Tennessee

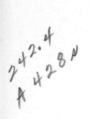

1. Meditations
I. Title

242.4
A 428 N

DEWEY DECIMAL CLASSIFICATION NUMBER: 242.4

Library of Congress catalog card number: 67-19395

Printed in the United States of America
5.JY6713

Preface

Thank you for opening this book. It was prepared with you in mind, as the crises of life are universal problems. If you do not need its message today, you will some day!

Nearly everyone would agree that life includes built-in hardships, for suffering comes to all mankind. We would also agree that in this conflict of circumstances many become bitter while others come forth from the fire better persons.

This book deals with the great crises of life. It speaks to that one who sincerely searches for a solution to the shadows through which he walks—the problems he experiences in living with himself and others. When life tumbles in . . . the Christian faith always offers a rainbow of God's presence and promise.

My deep gratitude to W. J. Fallis and William S. Cannon of Broadman Press and to Mrs. Alfred A. Brian, Jr., and Miss Arline Harris for their help with the manuscript.

R. Earl Allen

for
the memory of
Norma Alline

and for
the love of
Norma Joyce
James Todd
Joy Earline

who have brought
. . . . sunshine into shadows

Contents

Contents

1
Beyond the Shadow of a Doubt

A man shall be as an hiding place from the
wind, and a covert from the tempest; as rivers
of water in a dry place, as the shadow of a
great rock in a weary land.   Isaiah 32:2

"I have never had a shadow of a doubt," we have heard
people say. Yet every life has known some shadow—even
the shadow of a doubt. There are times in our lives when
God works through shadows as well as sunshine. Many
profitable lessons can be learned from such experiences.

We easily associate God with thunder, lightning, and
wind; we rarely think of associating him with shadows. But
it is a word we find often in the Bible, as in the familiar
twenty-third Psalm: "Yea, though I walk through the valley
of the shadow" (v. 4). We are fearful when darkness comes
over us, but our spiritual eyes are strangely capable of seeing God more clearly in the shadows than in the glare of
sunlight.

The word *shadow* has gained many emotional connota-
tions with the passage of time. It has become a strongly de-
scriptive word in the English language. A shadow has no
weight; it is thin and evasive. "The rainbow is a part of
God's law," said Thomas Jefferson, "and so is the Milky
Way, and so is the shadow of a child." It is true that a
shadow is just as fidgety as a little child, constantly in
movement, ever out of our reach.

Yet shadows have mighty influence. The Creator of this
universe said of his handiwork when he finished that it

was good. His creation included not only the sun but also
the shadows. Shadows have beauty. Artists have told us that
without them a picture would be very poor indeed. Shadows give definition, focus, and depth. When in their proper
places, light is accentuated and images stand out in proper
perspective. This is also true in our lives. Shadows teach us
many things, especially gratitude for and enjoyment of
the blessings God sends us.

It is frequently said that these are the most strenuous
times mankind has ever known. But the shadows of stress
and sorrow are not new. They have been part of human
life from the beginning. Doubt is not new. The tempter
planted doubt in Eve's mind: "Yea, hath God said?" The
result of giving in to doubt has plagued us since the day
Adam and Eve heard God say, "In the sweat of thy face
shalt thou eat bread" (Gen. 3:19).

Many of the things that frustrate us also troubled the
saints throughout the centuries. As we read of them in
God's Word, we find that God has an answer for every
problem in every age. His word for them and for us is
the same. "Behold, a king shall reign in righteousness, and
princes shall rule in judgment. And a man shall be as
an hiding place from the wind, and a covert from the tempest; as rivers of water in a dry place, as the shadow of a
great rock in a weary land" (Isa. 32:1-2).

When the Bible says that a man is "as the shadow of a
great rock in a weary land," it is referring to the Lord
Jesus Christ, the promised Messiah. Through him alone
is perfect rest available. The shadow of his cross gives protection from evil.

How pleasant it is on a day of hot sunshine to take refuge
under a tree that stands tall, whose branches provide cool
shade. But some areas of our world have no trees. Part of

Palestine is a barren, rocky land and its climate provides the basis for many Bible illustrations.

In the desert, a man has to seek refreshment and rest in the shadows cast by gigantic barren rocks. God describes his Son as being such a resting-place, the shadow of a mighty rock in a weary land, a refuge in a world that is feverish from its frustrations, a world that is weary with its problems, a world that finds no rest in itself. God sent his Son to provide for us safety and refuge in such a world.

Before clocks were invented, men made sundials and placed them where the shadow cast by the sun would tell them the time of day. Muhammad, the great Arabian prophet, could not carry a sundial with him as he traveled across the desert, but he needed to know the time of day so that he could prostrate himself toward his holy city at the hour of prayer. He learned to judge the time by standing up against the sun and measuring his shadow; when his shadow was a certain length, it was time for him to pray.

We may not pray at such special times, but the shadows of our lives teach us to pray, for when they come we feel the need of prayer more than we do at other times. At one time or another, some shadow has fallen across the mind and heart of every person prompting him to seek God.

In trying to describe the problems of mankind, Shakespeare said, "Life's but a walking shadow," meaning it was empty, transient. The Bible gives a positive answer to the riddle of life. Jesus Christ said, "I am the resurrection and the life," and the apostle John wrote, "He that hath the Son hath life."

But the shadows of life are nevertheless real. One little boy may have spoken more truth than he knew when he was questioned about his brother who, during World War II, was stationed in the Aleutian Islands off Alaska. When someone asked him where his brother was, the boy replied, "In the Illusion Islands." That is where many people dwell: in a land of unreality, where life is nothing more than a shadow, a dream, an illusion; and doubts are more real than faith. Such an attempt to escape the reality of life's shadows is futile.

Suspicion

Even the shadow of a doubt can sometimes be profitable. A doubting question may turn out to be a constructive question. The big problem lies in defining the word *doubt*. There are doubts that arise from a suspicious mind. Other doubts arise in open minds that are seeking evidence, searching for truth. When Jesus came at an early age into the Temple, he sat down with the teachers and questioned them concerning their knowledge. In turn, they questioned him, because they doubted his maturity; yet they were amazed at his understanding. Doubts and questions frequently challenge our thinking.

In the life of John the Baptist there came a time when, doubting, he asked an important question. When Jesus came to him to be baptized, this mighty preacher of repentance declared, "He must increase and I must decrease." Later, while languishing in prison, he sent one of his followers to ask Jesus, "Art thou he that should come, or do we look for another?" (Matt. 11:3).

Today many ask concerning Jesus, "Is he the Son of God, or shall we look for another?" Others seem to take pride in their doubts. Is not God beyond doubt? Although this is an age of questions, when we deal with God we are dealing with the Absolute! He is beyond doubt! If God is, he remains the same yesterday, today, and forever. The current attack which claims that God is dead may be contemporary, but it is not new. He has always remained victorious over his would-be pallbearers.

During his ministry, Jesus saw many of his followers departing and asked his disciples, "Will ye also go away?" Peter answered, "Lord, to whom shall we go? thou hast the words of eternal life" (John 6:67-68). Only the Lord Jesus Christ is the great rock in a weary land that provides refreshing, strengthening, protecting shadows. We need not look for another, because in him we find complete solace and perfect rest. When we fully recognize the needs of our own souls, we know that only God has the answer.

"See, it is the Lord!" cried Simon Peter joyously from the boat on the stormy Sea of Galilee. Impulsively he jumped out and walked across the water to meet his Master. But a few steps later, perhaps for the first time realizing what he was attempting, he looked down and saw the insubstantial waves under his feet. He began to sink and called out to Jesus for help.

"O thou of little faith," Jesus rebuked him, catching him by the hand, "wherefore didst thou doubt?" (Matt. 14:31). Peter had been looking in the wrong place for security. It was not in the substance under his feet, but in the power of his Lord. Peter looked at his doubt, and his faith faltered.

Chronic Complaint

The same rebuke comes to all of us when our faith falters. God says, "Why did you doubt me? When did you begin to question my power?" Did the doubting question grow out of eagerness to know more of God? Or was it just chronic complaint?

Is it honest questioning, or merely a subterfuge to escape God's holy demands? When we continually nurse a doubt and deliberately take refuge in questionings, we are headed for serious trouble, not only spiritually, but possibly physically.

"This mind and this body of ours live so close together," said Talmadge, a great preacher of a past century—before Freud—"that the disease of one affects the other." Responding with chronic complaints to the situations of life, a man can develop bitterness of soul which can be just as destructive to the body as cancer.

The God who made us, and his Son of whom it was said that he "needed not that any should testify of man: for he knew what was in man" (John 2:25), have instructed us how to diagnose our doubts and how to handle our intellectual problems. With our faith in him, we are to rejoice in all things. Only God can give inner peace, that mysterious medicine which no earthly source can provide to soothe the mind and comfort the aching heart.

A Christian may ask honest intellectual questions, of course! But he should not "fail of the grace of God; lest any root of bitterness springing up trouble [him], and thereby many be defiled" (Heb. 12:15). God warns us that such things are infectious. Bitterness in the heart of a father will boil over into the heart of his son. Doubt in the heart of a family will infect the church and community. God's Word instructs us not to let the seeds of bitterness grow in our hearts, lest they defile us and others.

Just as the sun dries up life from the arid desert, so doubt and suspicion dry up the spiritual life. The growing, questioning minds of children are delightful. Children are never suspicious. Doubt is something they learn as they grow in experience with the ways of this world and lose their freshness from the hand of God.

We may seek to justify our negative attitudes by saying

that it is "the Dutch in us," or "the Irish in us," or "our southern blood." But is it not the sin in us? We become the architects of our own souls and personalities by the things we permit to shape us. Suspicion, doubt, and resentment, stirred up and built up, expand like rank-growing vines that can in time tear down all but the sturdiest buildings.

By scientifically controlled experiments it has been determined that over a period of time enough anger can be built up in an animal's brain to destroy eighty of his own species. In our respectable society, poison in an individual's mind may not physically endanger another, but it damages him.

For every shadow that falls across their lives, some people try to blame someone else. Then they build up a checklist of grudges and try to "get even." But it is impossible to get even with those who injure one, because if he deliberately wrongs another, he is far worse off than the one he means to punish.

The inevitable shadows of life are never helped by chronic complaining against either God or man. To be useful, shadows must be accepted through faith in God.

Confident Contentment

About the shadows that come across our lives, the things about which we are tempted to complain and doubt, God says, "Fret not thyself because of evildoers, neither be thou envious against the workers of iniquity" (Psalm 37:1). "Love your enemies" was the terse command of Christ.

This is one of the most difficult things in life to practice. It rules out doubt and suspicion and resentment toward others, as far as God's approval is concerned. We are not to fume away our lives over the calamities that may come. We should not read the troubling experiences of life as though they were the handwriting of God. They are not his word to us.

He loved us and sent his Son to save us. We need to find what he would have us do about ourselves and the world we live in. There is security in feeling that all is in God's hands—and so it is. But we are tempted to proceed to a false assumption that therefore we do not need to do anything about it — but he says we do!

The apostle Paul best exemplifies the perfect balance between confident contentment and energetic purpose. His unity with God by faith gave him refreshment and strength that enabled him to do more than perhaps any man of any generation.

"I have learned," Paul declared, "in whatsoever state I am, therewith to be content" (Phil. 4:11). Even in the shadows of great persecution, his faith in God kept him from doubt and fear. At the same time, he constantly pressed "toward the mark for the prize of the high calling of God in Christ Jesus" (Phil. 3:14).

It has been well said, "Feed your faith and your doubts will starve to death." Paul kept his faith well nourished in fellowship with God, through prayer and service. His life contained no lasting shadow, only the refreshing shade of that "mighty rock." He had not a shadow of a doubt about his Lord, no resentment against those who persecuted him, and a mighty love for those who had not heard the gospel. He dwelt in the hiding place of the Lord, safe from the wind and tempest, kept strong by God's Word and refreshed as with a spring in the desert.

In such an oasis there could be no fear or frustration, no apprehension or panic, no suspicion or doubt. "Peace I leave with you, my peace I give unto you," said the Lord Jesus Christ to his disciples on his last night with them.

2
Formula for Failure

Wherefore seeing we also are compassed about with so great a cloud of witnesses, let us lay aside every weight, and the sin which doth so easily beset us, and let us run with patience the race that is set before us.

Hebrews 12:1

In a northern orchard a vacationing minister noticed some apple trees which were so burdened down with fruit that they had to be propped up.

"What is the secret?" he asked the apple-grower. "How do you grow them so successfully?"

"I can't explain why," the orchard owner said, "but I can tell you what happened." He led the preacher to the base of a large tree and asked, "You see this mark?"

Close to the base of the tree was an ugly scar which had partly healed over through many years. "Yes, I can see it has been damaged. How did that happen?"

"In the beginning," the grower explained, "too much of the tree was going to wood and not into fruit. We found that if we scarred the tree, we got less wood and more fruit. And we're in the fruit business."

God has to let shadows fall on us and inflict scars across our lives, many times, to produce fruit. He is also in the fruit-growing business, the character-building business. God is preparing us for another world rather than making us comfortable in this one.

Perhaps it is more important in our day than it has ever

been before that we should stop and reevaluate what really counts in life. Success has become such a cult; formulas abound, filling many books. Most people are more interested in "the ten commandments for success" than they are in the Ten Commandments of God.

The thoughts and aspirations of modern man are geared to getting on top of the heap. The prevalent pattern of thinking does not take into consideration that some might make important contributions to the world without being number one. It is thought by some that you *must* be a success—otherwise the world will pass you by.

On a TV program called "Meet the Critics," someone who was asked to evaluate a new book made a discerning observation. "The problem is," he said, "that the author has made no room for failure. The book is written as if there were no heavy experiences in our lives, as if there were no problems at all. The theory seems to be that you must simply inhale and say, 'I am getting better all the time.'"

Serious spiritual and emotional problems arise from such attempts at rationalization. It is recognized that drugs, liquor, and even tobacco, are detrimental to our minds and bodies. But there are other poisons—mental and emotional—which are hazards to life and health. Many kinds of damage may be self-inflicted that lead to failure in every sense of the word.

One of the damaging things in our world is the fact that success has been defined only in terms of accumulation of wealth or fame. Our society in general seems to think it is all right to tread roughshod on any individual who does not measure up to its standard of success. The demands and expectations of the world are far removed from what God counts as success or failure in human life. He has set forth in the Bible a different standard by which he judges men.

"Ye have not chosen me," the Lord told his disciples, "but I have chosen you, and ordained you, that ye should go and bring forth fruit, and that your fruit should remain" (John 15:16). "Every branch in me that beareth not fruit he taketh away: and every branch that beareth fruit, he purgeth it, that it may bring forth more fruit" (v. 2).

What God rewards as success and what he condemns as failure are altogether different from the popular opinions of this world. For instance, an achievement award may be given to a man who has gained prominence in public life, yet secretly his own household considers him a failure in his relationships with his wife and children, or even his servants and associates.

On the other hand, home problems can minimize a man's working achievements. Two men went to work in a factory on a day when there was snow on the ground, and they were bundled up against the severe weather. One of them, because he was working in the boiler room, took off his overshoes, hung up his overcoat and jacket, and prepared himself for the job at hand. The other man, similarly removing his outer clothes, sat down at his desk and took up his responsibility of cost analysis. But he made some serious mistakes which almost lost him his job because he had brought with him certain burdens from home which prevented his concentration on his job. It wasn't as easy for him to strip himself of his mental burdens and put them in a locker, and he became as inefficient as if the other man had tried to work by the furnace in his overcoat.

Many people, because of the various shadows of life which seem ever present, think that the only way to cope with life is to take an attitude of resignation. The Spartan code is the best the world can offer—keep a stiff upper lip and ignore your problems. Some cynics refer to life as a rat race and consider a sense of frustration an inevitable part of it. Such people do not even dream of conquering life. They do not expect to rise above their problems, to reach a goal. They try to resign themselves to the status quo. They do not believe in any heroism or unselfishness; they give up!

Organic disease causes physical suffering, we know. Perhaps even more of the suffering on this earth, especially in our day, is caused by the failures that gnaw away at people. Men and women are haunted by the ghosts of their dead dreams when they do not measure up as they would like to for the sake of their community image, or perhaps for the sake of their family name.

Fear of Failure

"The worst thing we have to fear is fear itself," said the late President Franklin D. Roosevelt. Fear has become a destructive beast preying upon mankind. The built-in desire for success, the great human yearning for approval, brings continual conflict and pressure in the hearts and lives of men. Even the spotlight of success creates the shadow of the fear of failure.

This is true in children as well as in adults, and has been throughout civilization. It is said that Louis Pasteur, who became a famous scientist, was a mediocre student. In his day, little summary notes were written home to the parents. "He is the smallest boy in my class," his teacher wrote. "He is the least brilliant boy in my class. He has made the least progress of anybody this year." His father wondered whether it was worth the cost to send Louis away from home for further training. In the first letter home, the boy wrote, "Just be patient and trust me. I'll do better as I go on." One of his greatest steps toward success was overcoming his fear of failure.

"Go down to Egypt," God commanded Moses, whom we remember as the great lawgiver of God. Moses tried to refuse, saying that he could not speak clearly. What made Moses stutter and stammer? Possibly fear? At least, he argued with God that he was inadequate for such leadership and would only fail. Moses was haunted by the same causes of stress and strain that bring pressure in all our lives.

"The spirit, mind, and body together must be considered by the physician before he can bring about a complete recovery," said a speaker at a Johns-Hopkins University commencement. "It used to be that the physician was interested only in healing the disease. Now he realizes that he must heal the whole man or that which was functional can become organic."

Certainly the Great Physician is no less interested in a total diagnosis of our problems when we bring them to him. "Wilt thou be made whole?" Jesus asked a crippled man. The Bible tells us this man had been lying there helpless some thirty-eight years, and he needed a completely new pattern of life and relationships.

Sometimes we hear people claim that they love souls. Yet their actions demonstrate that they don't really like the people they say they are trying to win. There is a lack of love for the whole person; and a human being cannot be divided. Each personality is an integral whole. It is true that we shall have a different body to live in one day, but each will be recognizable, for personality and spirit are more basic and distinctive than physical appearance.

On one occasion I was waiting in a hospital with the family of a deacon who was undergoing unusually delicate and difficult surgery. "Your Dad is one of the great men I have known," I said to one of the grown sons, "one of the great saints of God."

The son, himself a church leader, replied, "You know, our problem is we are not making saints like that anymore."

That father would have been called a failure by the world. He was a humble farmer who most of his life had worshiped in a small, one-room church for which he sacrificed much. But his son knew that he had lived a wholesome and successful life.

Is it true that we are not making saints like that any more? We do not seem to have time for the long, slow ripening of godly character. We wake up to the thud of the morning paper hitting the front door. At breakfast we catch up on the horrors that overtook the world while we slept. It is easy to go to bed listening to the late news which recounts the disasters that happened during the day instead of committing ourselves to the Lord in prayer that God might give us peaceful and restful sleep. The rush of our modern world not only creates the fear of failure but seemingly tries to insure failure in living a life pleasing to God.

Finality of Failure

The fear of failure causes great pressure in life. But does failure have to be permanent? Does it have to be the end? No. Sometimes we learn more from failure than we do from success. Determination can make failure into stepping-stones. When Disraeli rose to speak in the English parliament for the first time, he was met with titters of amusement. He sat down in chagrin, murmuring to himself with resolve, "I shall rise again to speak." Few men have ever spoken to parliament more powerfully than he did in his later years. He twice became prime minister and close confidant of Queen Victoria. Not even Gladstone nor Churchill was more respected than he in his day.

Disraeli, as many other great men in the political realm, was one of the late-blooming people. Herbert Hoover was defeated overwhelmingly, yet never became embittered because of the things that were said about him. In his later years he was honored as one of the great elder statesmen of the land.

Early in life many people demand everything—right now! One young woman was totally unprepared to make a living when her father lost the family fortune. At nineteen, she was a social butterfly, spoiled and selfish. Her old friends departed and all the things she valued in life seemed lost. She jumped from a hotel window leaving a note which read, "I was made for caviar and all I can find is cabbage."

It is possible to be more truly serene in the shadows than in the sunlight. Sometimes in "cabbage" we can find understanding of this life of blood, sweat, toil, and tears. That is how the world is, after all—full of heartaches rather than success. In the shadows we are often forced to meditate, while in the sunlight we tend to bask in our own glory and enjoy the glare of the ego. Pride and self-confidence do not add up to success on God's chart. His criterion is fruitbearing, and for that the apple trees often need to be scarred.

Forgiveness of Failure

How, then, can we cope with the shadow of failure? How can we conquer the fear and stresses of life?

"There is no fear in love," Jesus declared, "but perfect love casteth out fear: because fear hath torment" (1 John 4:18). Love can cancel out our failures. God will not remind us of them. When we come to the Lord, we cease having to justify ourselves; in the prayer closets of our lives we do not have to pretend.

After all, sin is the greatest failure in his sight. The most

common translation of the Greek word for *sin* is *failure*. It
means we have missed the mark, we have "come short of
the glory of God" (Rom. 3:23). He offers full and free forgiveness in Jesus Christ. We need to bring to the Lord all
the sins we have not shared with him before, all those
things we have never confessed. He has promised to loose
the cords of frustration, pour ointment on the resentments
and hurts, and erase all the failures.

"The garment of humility is for you" is a wise old saying. "The mantle of charity is to cover your neighbor. Do
not get them mixed." Love cancels out sin, and forgiveness
is free to faith.

"Let us lay aside every weight," exhorted the apostle
Paul, "and the sin which doth so easily beset us"—the resentments, the strife, the doubt—"and let us run with patience the race that is set before us" (Heb. 12:1).

Therefore the shadow of failure need not haunt us. We
need not fear it; God is always ready to forgive the re-
pentant. And if we stand uncondemned before him, the
opinion of the world should not matter to us. As the old
song goes, "He'll understand, and say, 'Well done!'"

3
Struggles of Sin

*For this cause, when I could no longer for-
bear, I sent to know your faith, lest by some
means the tempter have tempted you, and
our labour be in vain.*   1 Thessalonians 3:5

It is a thrill to see children stand at attention and hear
them give the pledge of allegiance to the flag of the United
States of America, a symbol more meaningful than ever
in such a day as ours. For this flag was not born without a
struggle.

The author of "The Star-Spangled Banner," Francis Scott
Key, was a hymn writer who, as a civilian, involved himself
in the War Between the States. Rowing out to an enemy
ship to plead for a friend who was being held prisoner, he
himself was detained. All through the night, on that enemy
vessel, he could feel the shaking of the boat as the cannons
were fired. He watched as the shells burst on the shore.
In the morning he was anxious to know the outcome of the
battle, and the only sign that the fort still held out was the
flag flying above it. From his pocket he took an old envelope
and wrote down the words that have become our national
anthem. It ends with a question that has rung through the
years. Does that flag still wave? Is the cause unsurrendered?

The struggle for independence has continued through the
years and the battle to uphold the Constitution still goes
on. At Gettysburg, Lincoln stated it: "The struggle for a
more perfect union goes on." That which affects the nation affects all its individual citizens. In suffering and trial

both the nation and the church bring forth their harvest.
"As soon as Zion travailed," said the prophet Isaiah, "she
brought forth her children" (66:8).

The Testing of Character

In the early days of preaching the gospel message, the
apostle Paul was concerned about the needs of the young
church he had planted at Thessalonica, and he sent Timothy
to minister to the Christians there. He realized they would
be going through many testings. "I am concerned about
your safety," he was saying. "I knew that tests were bound
to come, possibly some tests that you would not be able to
bear. Would the struggle be too much for you? I am anxious
to know."

The same testings still exist in our day; the struggle
against sin continues unceasingly. This is true in the world,
in the nation, in the church, and in the individual life.

A recent magazine article described how a certain TV
commercial illustrating protection was made. Ducks have
waterproof feathers which enable them to swim and dive
without sinking. But men took a "wetting agent" and poured
it over a duck to destroy his natural waterproofing. Then
he was turned loose in the water. When he found that he
was sinking, that he could no longer swim, frustration set
in. He floundered in utter panic when he was not able to
keep his head above water.

Men were created to swim and dive successfully in the
waters of life but sin, like the "wetting agent," has destroyed our natural, created righteousness and we find ourselves up to our necks in the problems of life that threaten
to overwhelm us. We find ourselves hopelessly frustrated
unless we discover some way of gaining victory over sin.

It is instinctive to struggle, but sometimes we pause and

wonder if it is worth the effort. Why should we continue to resist, we ask ourselves, and frustration floods our hearts. "Would we were like animals," mused the poet Walt Whitman, observing the difficulties of man, knowing human frustrations, and noticing the tranquility of animals, "for I have not seen animals weep in the night because of the guilt of their sins. I have not seen them pour out their lives in remorse."

Yes, animals seem to live without worry, but they do not put words together and make poetry, even out of their frustrations. Animals can make only a limited contribution to the world. And when strain and tension are removed from human life, often we do not strive. In battling our fears and frustrations it is possible to rise above them in victory. Out of man's troubles, in the awareness of his own soul, he rises to the heights of heroism and poetry.

This is even more true in the Christian life. We can count on divine help in our struggle against temptation and sin. But we must recognize that our enemy, Satan, is powerful, and we will have to engage in the moral and spiritual exercise of resisting him all of our days.

The apostle Paul went as far as to say, "We glory in tribulations also: knowing that tribulation worketh patience; and patience, experience; and experience, hope" (Rom. 5:3-4). There are many things we need to learn in the process of living. Through tribulation we learn patience; in patience we acquire experience; through experience we gain greater hope and stronger faith in the God who has proved himself in our lives. Thus, trials contribute to the character of the individual and the stamina of the group.

God has a purpose for us in this struggle against sin. As exercise builds muscles, struggle builds character.

It seems that our world today is not so much interested in character as it is in camouflage. We have tried to substitute cleverness for character. We have come to the place where we no longer feel that a man has to know some*thing;* he has to know some*body!* No longer is it necessary for a man to be something; he must be clever enough to get someone to do something for him. We should strive to overcome the tribulations that beset us. The struggle strengthens our faith and brings victory in our lives.

The Lord "is like a refiner's fire" declared the prophet Malachi in vivid simile. "And he shall sit as a refiner and purifier of silver, and he shall purify the sons of Levi, and purge them as gold and silver, that they may offer unto the Lord an offering in righteousness" (3:2-3).

When a manufacturer advertises his product, he frequently guarantees it. How is he able to do that? Because it has been put through certain rigorous tests. An automobile tire, for instance, is subjected to extremely rough usage to see whether it will stand the abuse of high speed and poor roads. Only after tests have been made can a guarantee be offered.

Temptation itself is not sin, it is only a test. Sin is the failure to pass the test successfully. Our Lord encountered all the problems that we have. The Bible tells us that he was "in all points tempted like as we are, yet without sin" (Heb. 4:15). He did not succumb to temptation; he did not fail the tests. His guarantee was written in his resurrection after the exhaustive test of Calvary had been made.

During his ministry he spoke about the tests of life in a now familiar story of two men who built houses. As he concluded the Sermon on the Mount he said of the man who would heed his words, "I will liken him unto a wise man, which built his house upon a rock . . . and it fell not: for it was founded upon a rock." He continued, "Every one that heareth these sayings of mine, and doeth them not, shall be likened unto a foolish man, which built his house upon the sand: and the rain descended, and the floods came, and the winds blew, and beat upon that house; and it fell: and great was the fall of it" (Matt. 7:24-27).

In a hospital one frequently hears a physician tell the family of a patient, "We do not know the exact nature of the illness or what the chances are of a quick recovery. Tests are still going on." In life, also, we do not yet know what we shall become because the tests are still going on.

The Conflict of Circumstance

"I wish I had never been made!" exclaimed a heavy-hearted woman to her pastor.

"You have not yet been made," he answered with loving understanding. "You are in the process of being made. That is what hurts."

Another said that she had prayed every morning for thirty years without being answered. "Every morning I get up with hope and pray for the Lord to make me good," she complained, out of her feeling of inadequacy, "and every evening I have had to kneel down and acknowledge my utter defeat." She was being answered, of course, and was growing spiritually as she persevered in the desire for holiness and acknowledged her failures daily to God. Frequently we feel that he does not hear and answer us when our good intentions are defeated by circumstances that weaken and tempt us.

The circumstances surrounding our lives affect us strongly and they influence our encounters with temptation. Not only the pattern of present-day living but the whole history of the world opposes us as we strive to live up to godly ideals.

Mankind has always longed for peace, but there has been almost continuous strife since the beginning of time. Observers say that in about five thousand years of recorded history, with the possible exception of about five hundred scattered years, mankind continuously has been involved in declared war. We are aware of the present reality of so-called "cold war" and the suffering caused by civil wars. The first man born into this world murdered his brother, and the results of selfishness and hate have continued through all the centuries.

Not all the struggle in life is physical or national; it comes also in the mental and moral realms. Today we are more aware than before of moral breakdown and its effect on society. Mental breakdown, also, is on the increase as a result of the continuing stresses and frustrations in human life. The battles of life are continuous.

We do not like to face this fact. We try to look for the easy way out. "Is there a pill you can take when you are tired?" one lad asked. We search for a way to avoid any crisis. Yet it is only through crisis that we develop character. "When the going gets tough," Coach Frank Leahy has been quoted as saying to his boys in the locker room, "let the tough get going!" Out on the playing field, as in life, tests are being made, the struggle is going on.

Temptation is inevitable, but it must not be invited! A scene in a novel echoed the one in the book of Job between God and Satan.

"Why did you dare tempt this young woman?" God asked.

Satan replied, "She came on my ground."

Consciously or carelessly, we come on Satan's ground. Jesus Christ taught his disciples to pray, "Lead us not into temptation." A wise saying further advises, "When you flee temptation, be sure you don't leave a forwarding address."

"What would you do if you were in this fix, Mr. Moody?" someone asked D. L. Moody, that great preacher of another generation.

"I would never have gotten into that fix to begin with!" said Mr. Moody. Although he might not have been following the counseling techniques considered proper today, he gave his honest opinion. He would have been aware that it was the devil's ground, and he would have stayed off it.

Early in life, Jacob became known as a liar and a deceiver, but he was always obsessed with a desire for the blessing of God. There came a time of momentous decision when he was struggling with the angel of God. "I will not let you go until you bless me," Jacob panted. The angel touched Jacob's thigh and Jacob limped the rest of his life, but he gained the blessing and a new name which meant "a prince with God." Regardless of whether or not we come out of our struggles with a limp or a scar, if we hold on to God and refuse to let go until he blesses us, until he enables us to conquer through the grace of the Lord Jesus Christ, we will have blessed victory!

The Solution at Calvary

Only at Calvary do we find the solution of the conflict with sin, and that on an individual basis. Some try to put their faith in other things. A "Letters to the Editor" column in a newspaper published a letter which said, "I predict that with our churches and their programs of Christian education, in another generation crime and evil will be abolished completely. With good parents and good environment, evil will disappear." Well-meaning—but wrong! Before we get through with one generation, the volunteer crop of sin increases in the next. The children are not gone until the grandchildren are here, and the struggle between good and evil continues in each life.

We have more churches—and more crime. Sin has a way of walking right in at the main gate. As the tree of temptation was in the midst of paradise, so it remains central in our daily lives. And its branches are like serpents reaching out to strike when we are weakest, when we are lonely, heavyhearted, hungry, tired. Even the Lord Jesus himself did not escape. After the endorsement of the Father at his baptism, "the Spirit led him into the wilderness," we are told, where he fasted for forty days. Then the tempter came!

The first temptation was physical. "If you are hungry, change these stones into bread—*if* you are the Son of God." The devil put it in such a way that it looked like Jesus was denying that he was the Son of God if he did not make bread out of the stones. But he who came to die on a cross could not stop to be a baker of bread.

Then Satan tempted him at mankind's most vulnerable point—vanity. He tempted Jesus with the easy way to the goal. That is where so many fall. We want to give up when the struggle gets hard! The last temptation also was to avoid the struggle—to gain the kingdoms of earth without the suffering that God deems necessary.

These were the same temptations that came to Eve—to satisfy physical appetite and to gain power and knowledge without having to strive for it. Like Eve, we still grasp for the brass ring, always trying to get something for nothing— the easy way.

When Jesus tried to tell us to love our enemies, he said we should love others as we love ourselves. He knew that if we did this, we would treat them with kindness and concern, and he set the example. Paradoxically, we also have the problem that even though we love ourselves, we fre-

quently become our own worst enemies, we love ourselves
so much.

The struggle for victory will never be easy. It was never
easy for the Son of God. In the garden of Gethsemane, he
struggled still with the forces of evil and against the temptation to complain that the way was too hard. The Bible says
that he was in agony. Yet he persevered with God's plan
and provided for us the way of escape. We suffer from the
effort and pain of struggle against sin, but he bore the sting
of it, the festering poison of sin itself to provide the anti-
dote, to provide the vaccine that keeps it from being fatal
to us.

"There hath no temptation taken you," the apostle Paul
assured us, "but such as is common to man: but God is faithful, who will not suffer you to be tempted above that ye are
able; but will with the temptation also make a way to
escape, that ye may be able to bear it." (1 Cor. 10:13).
There is always an emergency exit. Look for it!

"An idle mind is the devil's workshop" is more than an
ancient proverb. Paul tells us how to counterattack: "Be
not overcome of evil, but overcome evil with good" (Rom.
12:21). James counseled resistance, "Submit yourselves
therefore to God. Resist the devil, and he will flee from
you" (James 4:7).

Calvary is the only place where complete victory can be
won in the struggle against sin. It is ours for the taking;
and, it is the only way to true peace amid the conflicts of
life.

4
Learning to Loaf

He said unto them, Come ye yourselves apart
unto a desert place, and rest a while: for there
were many coming and going, and they had
no leisure so much as to eat.   Mark 6:31

A tribe in South America was famous for its hunting skill. Having very primitive equipment, they had to get close to an animal to secure it and they took pride in running fleetly.

On a Sunday, as a missionary approached their village for the first time, he found the men prostrate on the ground. He stopped and bowed his head respectfully. "What are they doing?" he asked his guide. Surely they were not praying, for these people had never even heard the Word of God.

Through an interpreter he was told that they said, "We wait after every hunt for ourselves to catch up." They ran so fast they felt they needed to wait for their spirits to catch up with their bodies. Unconsciously they were following God's pattern, for the Lord of creation made a day of rest.

How shall we find the right pattern for living? Has the schedule God provided become impractical in our day? Many people seem to think so. It is true that patterns of living have changed, and probably they will continue to change. In pioneer days, if a man missed a stagecoach, he could unwind before another came along the next week. There was an era when, if a man missed his train, he just passed the time until another came by the next day. Now we have stepped up the pace of life until, if we miss a section of a revolving door, we almost have a breakdown.

Our present-day difficulties, it is claimed, are brought about by the age in which we live. This is partly true, but some are a result of the past—rapid expansion, industrial revolution, and the generations that have gone before us. During the depression of the thirties many learned early that those who did not work did not eat. Activity became the watchword—keeping everlastingly at it, and its invisible scar remains. Laziness was the cardinal sin.

We fail to distinguish between "contentment" and "laziness." Some people never have learned that there is a difference, that relaxation between days is not the same as being lazy through the days. In some Christian circles, waiting on the Lord, being still and knowing that he is God, is not considered as worthwhile as effort and activity. Developing the virtues of peacefulness and patience is seldom recommended.

No man was ever more sought after than Jesus. Even his disciples were pressed by the crowds which struggled to get near him. A group of Greeks approached Philip, saying, "Sir, we would see Jesus" (John 12:21). "You are one of his disciples," they were saying. "See if you can get us in past this crowd. Perhaps if *you* would tell him that we would like an audience with him, he would make a way for us."

Many times children rushed up to Jesus. When his disciples, wanting to do the right thing, wanting to protect him, tried to push them away, he stopped his disciples with a command, "Bring them to me." His disciples thought the children were not very important, but Jesus was setting up a new scale of values in which he always had time for children.

On another occasion the disciples went into a Samaritan town to buy food. They left Jesus resting by the city well. A woman came to draw water and the Master engaged her in conversation. When the disciples returned, they could not understand why he should take the time to speak to a woman, why he should give up his rest to befriend her and meet her needs.

They broke open the lunch and spread food before him, but Jesus said, "I have meat to eat that ye know not of" (John 4:32). Great inner satisfaction, contentment, refreshment had come to him through doing the will of his Father and fulfilling the holy obligations of his life—renewed strength that nothing else could provide, not even food. We are God's creation. "We are his workmanship, created in Christ Jesus unto good works" (Eph. 2:10).

God provides wonderful spiritual refreshment for us as we do his bidding, but we are not to neglect our bodies foolishly or injure them. The apostle Paul summed up his lecture to the Corinthians on their physical appetites by saying, "What? know ye not that your body is the temple of the Holy Ghost which is in you, which ye have of God, and ye are not your own?" (1 Cor. 6:19). God himself dwells in us—how, we cannot understand, but his Spirit comes to inhabit this mortal frame of ours. "Therefore glorify God in your body, and in your spirit, which are God's" (v. 20). It is not only good sense, according to the pages of God's Word, it is good religion to keep the body strong and useful for God's glory.

One of the problems we face, trying to keep our bodies strong in these hectic days, is learning the fine art of relaxation. Everyone ought to be interested in it, although it is often an evasive goal.

Jesus understood this human need. Several times we read that he urged his disciples to come apart and rest a while. He who made man understands the whole man and all his interrelated needs. Jesus often was tired. He had to withdraw from the crowds to restore his own physical body and refresh his mind. He used such opportunities also to instruct his disciples. Soon he would withdraw from them, and they would have the total responsibility of directing his work.

To all mankind he expanded that invitation for rest and refreshment. "Come unto me," he said. "Take my yoke upon you. . . . For my yoke is easy, and my burden is light" (Matt. 11:28-30). Was not the invitation twofold? To the individual who staggers under a burden of sin, he holds out salvation. He offers to take that burden of guilt and despair instantly, replacing it with his forgiveness and peace. "Learn of me," he went on to say, "for I am meek and lowly in heart, and ye shall find rest unto your souls" (v. 29). This is our invitation into the blessedness of his continual tranquility.

Perspective

High value is set on activity and accomplishment, so much so that we find it difficult to pause and evaluate our lives. We do not intend to become so involved in the rush and lose peace of mind. Then why? We lack perspective!

Though it may be a shocking experience, a man needs to take a good look at himself occasionally. What kind of a person are we, anyway? What are the faults we need to correct? What are the abilities we need to strengthen? But it is even better that a man take a good look at God, for this is the vision that puts all things in proper perspective.

How can we see God if we do not take time to know him? In the present-day culture, few seem to be willing to give God three hours on the Lord's day out of the 168 hours in the week. Each one has a schedule so full he finds it hard to breathe, much less to breathe a prayer.

The God who knows us better than we know ourselves knew that we would face this particular temptation. He planned the calendar to provide a day of rest, and even wrote it into the law he gave to Moses for his people. Often a man finds an illness helpful, when he is forced to be still for a while.

In quietness we learn to value spiritual things above material things, and that is about the only time we ever do because we get so involved in this materialistic world. Our values so easily get lopsided that we shortchange eternal things for the sake of temporal things. "Why hurry?" someone has wisely said, "You are going to live forever—somewhere. So why rush?"

God's perspective makes us recognize that this mortal body will last only threescore and ten years—plus, if God gives us health and strength. Even fourscore years is not very long in comparison to eternity. How can we afford to neglect the spiritual factors of life that shall last forever? "What shall it profit a man," asked Jesus, "if he shall gain the whole world, and lose his own soul?" (Mark 8:36).

We need to put more emphasis on eternal values and let our temporal wants dwindle to a minimum. That is just the opposite of the philosophy of life in our present-day world. We are urged on every hand to satisfy our wants, and as we do, the desires grow. If we do not stop the spinning of the clock somewhere, what will happen to us? Breakdown or worse!

A wise old deacon in a rural church kept his wants from getting the best of his budget by a simple formula. "We go to town every Saturday," he said, "except those Saturdays when we can't afford to go. Then what we don't see we don't want, and everything is fine." His philosophy resulted in a certain peace of mind, but that was before "charge" was better than cash and before TV commercials took the place of door-to-door salesmen.

The answer can only be that selectivity is important in all areas of life. We cannot have everything, we must choose what is most important. Although we may tend to count material things more important in our own lives, we recognize and appreciate those who think in terms of other people. If we try to list the people who have had the greatest influence on our lives, we usually find that they have not put material things first.

We even have to choose what tasks to do and what to leave undone because we have so many requests for our time. The problem is that so often the good is the worst enemy of the best! We are pressured into doing good things for the world, good things for the community, even good things for the Lord's work, and we do not have time for the best things. We have to select what is most important if we want our lives to be worth something.

There are times when it is just as Christian to say no as it is to say yes. We have only so many hours to live, and eternity will judge us according to the use we make of them.

Patience

To select and accomplish the most important things in life takes not only perspective but patience. "For ye have need of patience," we are told in the New Testament, "that, after ye have done the will of God, ye might receive the promise" (Heb. 10:36).

For most of us, patience is the most difficult virtue to achieve. In a lighter vein it has been said that "patience is the ability to idle your motor when you feel like stripping your gears."

One day a doctor appeared in the door of a hospital room and, before he could speak, the patient burst out, "Let me say it. I have not yet learned to coast."

"Physician, heal thyself," the doctor retorted as he turned to leave.

"Wait a minute!" the patient called out. "There's a vast difference between a diagnosis and a cure!"

Our problem may be that we are in a hurry and God is not! That does not mean he is less interested. We have a built-in awareness of the limitations of time, but God has all the time in the world, plus eternity. We want to plant and harvest in the same hour. God does not schedule his divine work that way.

"I have planted," wrote the apostle Paul to the young churches of his day. "Apollos watered; but God gave the increase. So then neither is he that planteth any thing, neither he that watereth; but God that giveth the increase" (1 Cor. 3:6-7). This is the perspective of patience.

As a young officer, General Dwight Eisenhower learned many important lessons, as revealed in his autobiography. Up until the time his firstborn son was three years old, his most serious assignment seemed to be coaching football on an insignificant army post in Kansas. He felt he was not accomplishing anything, but General Carnegie told him that to learn of combat on the football field would be valuable to a commanding officer facing live ammunition. Of the death of his three-year-old child at that time, Eisenhower wrote, "Happiness is not always in the sunlight. Even the shadow can outline the image of God."

We need patience in developing communion and fellowship with God; that is very important and necessary. When we learn patience with ourselves and God, we can do great things. "The trying of your faith worketh patience," said James.

"But let patience have her perfect work, that ye may be perfect and entire, wanting nothing" (James 1:3-4).

Peace

Patience brings peace. "I have learned . . . to be content," declared the apostle Paul. Much of the wisdom of his later years was not given to him in stunning revelations like his Damascus road experience. He learned through the process of living and seeking God's will, through experience and suffering. But he expressed for us his great secret. "I know both how to be abased, and I know how to abound: every where and in all things I am instructed both to be full and to be hungry, both to abound and to suffer need. I can do all things through Christ which strengtheneth me" (Phil. 4:12-13). This is a great description of peace and patience. He had learned how to accept things as they are, the good with the bad. He did not fret over things he could not help.

Paul believed there was an eternal purpose in all things, even the frustrations and sufferings of this life. As a wise preacher in the Old Testament said, "To every thing there is a season, and a time to every purpose under the heaven" (Eccl. 3:1). Then he went on to list all the many things that happen to us in life. We should not take notice of just the outstanding things but also see the purpose in *all* things.

Paul trusted God completely. When Saul the Pharisee met the Lord Jesus on the Damascus road, he turned everything over to him: "Lord, what wilt thou have me to do?" (Acts 9:6). In his cloak was a list of those whom he was going to Damascus to persecute, but the list was no longer of any value.

Paul's doctrine of living can be described as "Acceptology, Tryology, Trustology, and Doxology." Paul tried, wherever he was, whatever he was doing, to do a good job for the Lord. Some have no peace because they are not trying to do anything for God or others. They are trying only to please themselves. "Stir up the gift of God, which is in thee," Paul instructed young Timothy (2 Tim. 1:6). "Be strong in the grace that is in Christ Jesus" (2:1).

Frequently it takes many failures to achieve success, and that takes perseverance. Sports fans can tell us that Babe Ruth hit 714 home runs, but they forget that he was also champion in striking out; he struck out 1,330 times! Had he not been in there trying, he would not have made all the home runs.

Paul also described several kinds of peace. He spoke of "the peace of God, which passeth all understanding" (Phil. 4:7). We have peace *with* God the moment we are saved. "Therefore being justified by faith, we have peace with God through our Lord Jesus Christ" (Rom. 5:1). When we have the peace of our salvation, this is peace with Christ, the result of a relationship which has been established.

There are a lot of believers who do not have the peace *of* Christ, for that is quite a different thing. We can have the peace of Jesus only by doing the will of God and majoring on the needs of others rather than on a desire for things.

The commonplace motto, "Jesus first, others second, self last," is still the secret of serenity.

5
Success

What things were gain to me, those I counted loss for Christ (Phil. 3:7). *These things have I spoken unto you, that my joy might remain in you, and that your joy might be full.*
John 15:11

"Nothing succeeds like success." This catch phrase, born of mankind's desire to achieve, has been repeated over and over, until it has become a powerful motivation for many people. Some take it as an answer to all the problems of life.

Secular standards of success are in direct conflict with spiritual standards. At one college commencement, the minister who spoke in the morning told the graduates, "Hitch your wagon to a star. Go out and dream great things and do great things." That evening the commencement speaker, a businessman who had not been at the morning service and who read from a manuscript already prepared, said to the same audience, "Be practical. Go out and do the practical thing at all costs."

Paradoxically, there was no real conflict between the two. Great ideas are necessary. Often they have moved men to put them to work in very practical ways. Sometimes it takes a generation for an idea to become practical; sometimes we have to wait for the time of doubt to pass. Sometimes a dream has to wait for its season—but it will come!

"Ideals are like stars," it has been said. "We never reach them, but like the mariners of the sea, we chart our course by them."

Eager young graduates are typical of people who go out in a hurry to make a success in life, to be somebody and to do something. Too often they do not really know just what success is supposed to be if they find it. Success is not just simply having an adequate stockpile; it is a specific quality of life as well.

In a sense it is a highly individual matter. What is success to you? What is important to you? Success is found, not in one's deeds, but in one's soul. Certainly success for a Christian must include following God's guidance and fulfilling God's purpose for his life.

Norman Thomas, the Socialist who ran for president many times over the years, said that to him the only verse in all the Bible that made sense was, "Seek ye first the kingdom of God, and his righteousness; and all these things shall be added unto you" (Matt. 6:33). Then he added, "I've wached Christianity for a long while. The other things don't seem to be added." What are the other things? What is it God wants us to have, what would he add to us? For these answers we must look into his Word, the Bible.

Spoils of Success

An archaic word found often in the Old Testament appears also in another modern phrase that is often repeated but seldom defined: "To the victor belong the spoils." What are spoils? The word came from ancient times when there were no commissioned, paid armies. The men who fought lived on the country through which they passed and they plundered villages and cities. They brought back with them everything movable: jewelry and clothing, sheep and cattle, even men, women, and children as slaves. The prophet Isaiah referred to the practice when he used the simile "as men rejoice when they divide the spoil" (9:3).

David decreed a new procedure for his warriors. "As his part is that goeth down to the battle," he said, "so shall his part be that tarrieth by the stuff: they shall part alike" (1 Sam. 30:24). This concept of giving all who worked for the cause a share in the victory is carried over into the New Testament by Jesus. "My peace I give unto you" (John 14:27), he said. "These things have I spoken unto you, that my joy might remain in you, and that your joy might be full" (John 15:11). "I am come that they might have life," he declared, "and that they might have it more abundantly" (10:10).

In Hebrews it is said of him, "Jesus the author and finisher of our faith; who for the joy that was set before him endured the cross, despising the shame, and is set down at the right hand of the throne of God" (12:2). This is a summation of the most successful life ever lived, although it does not correspond with what the world calls success.

The second most successful life described in the Bible is probably that of the apostle Paul. From his prison in Rome he summed up his life in the words: "I have fought a good fight, I have finished my course, I have kept the faith" (2 Tim. 4:7). He evaluated his life in terms of how he had lived rather than what he had achieved. To the end he carried a confident heart, full of rejoicing in Christ, although his contemporaries did not consider him a success.

Status-Seekers

Neither Jesus nor Paul possessed what we today call "status," in spite of the fact that one was the Son of God and the other a nobleman of his people. They neither conformed to the standards of success in their own society nor in ours.

Modern Americans have been indicted as "status-seekers" in Vance Packard's soul-searching book by that name. Madison Avenue seems to have more influence on people's lives today than does God's Holy Word. Seven billion dollars a year is spent on determining what is important. Countless times every day we are told what is best, what will last, what will make us more popular, what will be more convenient. Many people have learned to desire certain things, not because they really want them, but because they are status symbols.

This is a day of conformity. No one is supposed to disturb the status quo, to be too different. Mass-advertising theory seems to take it for granted that we are not capable of making up our own minds. Commercials act as sultry sirens of Satan to urge us toward status-seeking and soft living, in spite of the warnings, not only in the Bible, but in the sage sayings of the secular world. "We must always be sure that we do not succumb to the temptation of making a living rather than making a life," one practical philosopher has said. And another: "If the world loses any of its worth, it is only because some of us take from it more than we give."

In times past, it was simpler to be counted a success. To be a great warrior, one had only to go out and slay the giant and the battle was won permanently—that is, until the next giant came along. Success, like failure, is relative—never final, but continuous. "The rung of a ladder was never meant to rest upon, but only to hold a man's foot long enough to enable him to put the other somewhat higher."

Status is not synonymous with success, as some people seem to think. Success does not mean superiority or rulership or even fame. That kind of evaluation leads to bitter controversies. "Success is often hard to take," it has been wryly said, "—especially when it's the other fellow's."

The New Testament proclaims a different standard of behavior in what we call the Golden Rule: "Therefore all things whatsoever ye would that men should do to you, do ye even so to them" (Matt. 7:12). With so many conflicting voices telling us what to want and how to act and what it takes to succeed, how can we judge what is true success and how can we seek it as Christians? When we confuse status and superiority, worth and success, in our minds, our motivations become twisted and our sense of values an unsafe guide.

Secret of Success

What is success? What is the secret of it?

The word "success" is kin to the word "ambition," which literally means one who goes out and gets votes. This was its original meaning. In our time it would be one who gains approval or wins applause or one for whom the curtain falls and is brought up again.

Is there anything wrong with ambition? Let us look at it in the light of the Scriptures. Paul knew when he set his face toward Rome that he would die there—it had been prophesied. But steadfast determination is different from stubbornness. Knowing that he would lose his head on the chopping block, Paul still thought the message worth the price. Paul went to Rome with the gospel to proclaim, and in doing that he was successful, even though he died.

From his Roman prison, Paul wrote an urgent letter full of advice to young Timothy, who was in the formative years of his life's ministry. Paul pleaded with the young man that he should not be misguided by the allurements around him and that he should not panic, even though his "spiritual father" suffered martyrdom. Instead, the young minister should use the abilities and opportunities God gave him and strive earnestly, not for self-glory, but to establish God's glory. As Paul wrote to another young preacher, Titus,

"These things speak, and exhort, and rebuke with all au-
thority. Let no man despise thee" (2:15).

Unfortunately, our personal viewpoint on life is limited
by time and space and understanding. We view things tem-
porally. We view things circumstantially. We view things
conditionally. This is the only century in which we have
lived and we can experience only a small part of the earth at
a time. Our news commentators try to give us the broader
picture of our world, but in doing so they naturally express
only what they see from their own viewpoint. The viewpoint
of God is comprehensive, beyond our understanding. He has
been in every century and he knows all things simultane-
ously.

True success recognizes human limitations and the
achievement of overcoming them. In such a large and complex world, it is easy to feel that we do not count for much.
We are tempted to envy others who have the kind of success we think we want. We may even take the childish attitude that because we cannot blow as big a balloon as someone else, why should we play at all? We need to find goals
that are flexible and not rigid, because success is getting
satisfaction from our goals. We should not grieve life away
over opportunities that may never be ours, but use our limited scope of life to the best advantage.

The peril of ambition lies in self-centeredness which
makes the goal itself false and empty. We consider Judas
the epitome of failure because, although involved in a divine cause, his motivation at last revealed itself as sheer
greed. When he saw what he had done, he tried to back
away, tried to return the thirty pieces of silver to the priests.
"What is that to us?" they sneered at him. "See thou to
that" (Matt. 27:4). "We don't want it back; you will have
to jingle it the rest of your days." Judas had the opportunity

of being honored down the centuries, along with the other faithful disciples, but his self-centered love of money made his name notorious as a traitor.

Judas could not join us, as would the other disciples, in singing a favorite modern song that reflects the joy of success for a Christian:

> I've discovered the way of gladness,
> I've discovered the way of joy . . .
> When I found Jesus, my Lord.

But as we sing it, do we actually believe it? Do we feel that we have truly found the way of life and joy? Success in life is not always a song you can sing, of course. There are the quieter joys of service and satisfaction and confidence.

"There are no secrets of success," someone has said. "It is doing the things you know you should do. It can as easily be not doing the things you know you should not do." Success is spending life in the best way, in the plan and providence of God, knowing that it is God's approval at the end of the way that counts.

If there is a secret of success it is to be found in the implications of the word "service." One man said, "Service is the rent I pay for the space I fill."

Satisfaction of Servants

The apostle Paul's consuming ambition was to be a servant well-pleasing to God. He did not preach as though the world were on fire—he preached as though it were burning up! He himself was on fire with zeal for the Master he loved and the gospel he proclaimed. "Henceforth there is laid up for me," he confidently asserted in the last days of his life, "a crown of righteousness, which the Lord, the righteous judge, shall give me at that day" (2 Tim. 4:8). Paul's great ambition, his anticipated satisfaction, would be his Lord's "well done, thou good and faithful servant!"

In the final judgment of God, it is the character of a man that counts. Success does not mean superiority. We must not confuse worth with show nor let superficial things become the passion of our lives. The visible shell is not the meat of a man.

"The first time I was an agent," said a railroad president when asked to give a statement of what it meant to succeed, "some people came up to the window in the little southern town and I ignored them. I picked up some papers and busied myself with the Morse Code apparatus.

" 'Have you ever noticed,' I heard one of them say to the other, 'the smaller the station, the bigger the agent?'

"I learned a great lesson that day," the successful man added, "and I made up my mind that I would no longer try to get by on superficiality rather than genuine service."

It is a sad thing indeed that many people seem never to learn that lesson. All they get out of their work is their pay envelope. There should be deep and rewarding satisfaction in service, especially in the service of God. A Christian should mature in his effective service to others. As he grows older, he also should continue to grow in his relation to his Lord.

In the New Testament we read about an elderly priest named Simeon, who had served God in the Temple all his life. How long this was we do not know, nor do we know how long he had prayed for the deliverer of Israel to come. When Mary of Nazareth came into the Temple with her baby Son, Simeon gathered the child in his arms and felt richly rewarded. "Lord," he prayed in profound thanksgiving, "now lettest thou thy servant depart in peace, according

to thy word: for mine eyes have seen thy salvation" (Luke
2:29-30).

John the Baptist lost his head to Herod's executioner, but
he did not die a failure. "Among them that are born of
women," Jesus said when he received word of John's death,
"there hath not risen a greater than John the Baptist" (Matt.
11:11).

When David Livingstone packed up a little bag and left
London to go to Africa, people thought he was an unbal-
anced fanatic. Now, generations later, his name is a household word around the world. History recognizes that Livingstone accomplished great things for God, that he was a
success in his service to God.

The only time the word "success" appears in the King
James Version of the Bible is in the promise of God to
Joshua: "This book of the law shall not depart out of thy
mouth; but thou shalt meditate therein day and night, that
thou mayest observe to do according to all that is written
therein: for then thou shalt make thy way prosperous, and
then thou shalt have good success" (Josh. 1:8). One of the
prophets restated it later: "He hath shewed thee, O man,
what is good; and what doth the Lord require of thee, but
to do justly, and to love mercy, and to walk humbly with
thy God?" (Mic. 6:8).

The best success we can achieve is to trade our status-
seeking for the cross of Christ. "God gives his very best to
those who leave the choice with him." Our motivation makes
a difference. The path of self-serving leads to self-destroying
frustration. Or, like Paul, through dedicated service we can
find the satisfaction of an honored servant of God.

6
Age of Anxiety

God hath not given us the spirit of fear; but
of power, and of love, and of a sound mind.
                                              2 Timothy 1:7

Two plagues have come upon us in our time. Two problems have a paralyzing grip on the heart of our world—solicitude, being overanxious, and solitude, loneliness.

A picture captioned "The Face of America" appeared on the cover of one of our leading magazines. It had been taken at the intersection of two busy city streets. The people, evidently unaware of the photographer as they hurried along, revealed not one single smiling face. Is that the face of America? Is a frown our habitual expression in our unguarded moments? Is everybody unhappy?

To double-check the depressing revelation of that picture, a man was sent to the same intersection with a sack of one thousand silver dollars. He was instructed to stand there from sunup to sundown and give a dollar to anyone who came along looking happy, whether he was smiling or not. At evening the man trudged away, having passed out only 740 silver dollars. The rest of them remained in the sack.

Evidently our times are well labeled "the age of anxiety." Perhaps even more appropriately it has been called "the aspirin age." It is a social as well as an individual problem, because anxiety is a contagion that spreads like a virus. Frustration is passed on from one person to another, from parent to child, from friend to friend, from worker to colleague.

The word "worry" is derived from an old Anglo-Saxon word meaning to struggle or choke. It paralyzes us, as far as making a positive contribution to the world, almost as effectively as a hand on our windpipe. It spreads over our land like a miasma through mass communication as well as personal contact. "Worry," it has been said, "pulls tomorrow's cloud over today's sunshine." Thinking about our problems is necessary, but worry brings no solution.

On every hand we find advice on how not to worry. One of the current books is a tongue-in-cheek bit of advice called *How to Worry Successfully*. The author claims that if you want to worry successfully, you must put all your energy into it, focus on the problem, give no thought to anything else except that which you are worrying about, and not believe that anybody else may be fair or right.

One of the pertinent symbols of our age is the neon sign with its restless flashing off and on. Its hurrying changeableness reflects our modern lives. America's Number One killers of the present day seem to be the clock, the calendar, and the telephone. All are wonderful servants, but demanding masters!

"The race is not to the swift," said a wise old preacher in the book of Ecclesiastes, "nor the battle to the strong" (9:11). Why not? Because God is swifter and stronger than men, and victory is found—eventual, permanent victory—only on his side of the conflict.

Frustration of Fretting

Anxiety and worry lead to fretting, and fretting erodes both physical ability and spiritual strength. Faith and trust deteriorate in a climate of worry. And it is completely useless. Christ reminded his disciples, "Which of you by taking thought can add one cubit unto his stature?" (Matt. 6:27).

We might add inches to our girth, however, as medicine recognizes worrying as one cause of compulsive eating. It has other physical effects also, some painful and damaging; it can cause functional problems which may become organic.

"The thing which I greatly feared is come upon me," complained Job, "and that which I was afraid of is come unto me" (3:25). The Bible tells us that what we think influences what we will become and that the subjects we dwell upon mold us into conformity.

That little-known but often-quoted writer of prose and poetry called Anonymous is reported to have said, "Don't borrow trouble; the interest on the loan will break you!" An old fable tells about a conversation between a robin and a sparrow concerning the way men hurry and worry. "Perhaps," said the robin, "they have no Heavenly Father such as cares for you and me." Our worrying dishonors God.

Bishop Quale, an aged preacher of another century, sat up very late one night worrying. Finally he seemed to hear a voice say to him, "Quale, you have worried long enough. You go on to bed now and I'll watch over the world the rest of the night." Surely the great God of the universe is capable of taking over the night shift! His eyes go to and fro upon the earth continually. We are told also, "He that keepeth thee will not slumber" (Psalm 121:3).

When the Babylonians conquered Jerusalem, they took from the house of God valuable vessels designed to be used in the worship of God. These they defiled and corrupted at their pagan feasts. At last, God wrote his condemnation on the wall of a Babylonian palace with a supernatural hand, and the empire fell that very night.

In later days there have been vandals who went into Jewish synagogues and put evil markings on the walls, desecrating the houses of God. Retribution was a long time coming, but it came. When anyone takes that which is dedicated to the worship of God and misuses it, God will not tolerate the situation indefinitely. Righteous people, also, should rise up in indignation against sacrilegious and unholy actions.

God raises a question in his Word which draws a powerful parallel. "What? know ye not that your body is the temple of the Holy Ghost which is in you?" (1 Cor. 6:19). If the body is the dwelling place of the Spirit of God, any misuse of that temple will be judged by God. We must not jeopardize that which is set apart as his property. Worry, solicitude, and much anxiety damage our bodies, and the Bible says that anything which weakens the temple of God offends the Spirit of God who inhabits it. Yet this body is not our permanent home.

We can say with Paul, "We know that if our earthly house of this tabernacle were dissolved, we have a building of God, an house not made with hands, eternal in the heavens" (2 Cor. 5:1). Our Saviour reassured us that he is coming back for us, "that where I am, there ye may be also" (John 14:3). No man who trusts Christ has reason to fear or fret, for his body and soul are in the hands of a great God! We can take courage; we can lean upon our faith with assurance. "My times are in thy hand," declared the psalmist (31:15). If our lives are committed to God's keeping, what cause can there be for worry?

"Fret not thyself because of evildoers" (Psalm 37:1) is the command of God to us. There is nothing we can do about them anyway. It is hard to trust and pray if we worry at the same time. Fretting is not only a harmful habit but the Bible declares it is sinful: "For whatsoever is not of faith is sin" (Rom. 14:23). Christ several times rebuked his disciples for their lack of faith. When they became fearful

in the storm on Galilee and awakened him, he chided, "Why
are ye fearful, O ye of little faith?" (Matt. 8:26). They
feared the storm until they realized that their safety de-
pended, not on the ship, but on the Saviour who was with
them in the ship.

Freedom from Fear

What can be done about fear? How can we escape it? Is
there any freedom from it?

Yes, but only when we use God's prescription. "The only
sovereign cure is trust in God," said William James, one of
the early pioneers in the field of psychology, though he himself claimed no personal faith. Nothing is more energy-
dissipating than inner conflict. Overanxiousness can render
our lives ineffective in many ways.

Only two fears are native to mankind, we are told: fear
of noise and fear of falling. All others are acquired, so we
ourselves are responsible for them. If we choose, we can
sabotage ourselves with worry until we cannot even live a
normal life.

Our word "sabotage" comes from the French word for
wooden shoe—sabot. If a workman wanted to break down
the factory where he worked, he would take off his wooden
shoe and throw it into the machinery. When we fret and
worry, we cast our own shoe into the functional machinery
of living and wreck our lives. "Whether it's a man or a motor," it has been said, "you can be sure something's wrong
with it if you hear it knocking."

Fear began in the Garden of Eden. God walked in the
cool of the day with the man and woman he had created.
One day they did not meet him at the appointed time and
place. Imagine the voice of Jehovah God echoing through
the green halls of Paradise as he lifted his voice and called,

"Adam, Adam, where art thou?" When Adam's hiding place was discovered, he confessed, "Lord, I was afraid." Having disobeyed God, he became afraid of him.

In the New Testament, Jesus told a parable about a wealthy man who gave his servants money to invest. On the day when the master asked for an accounting, the one who had been given five talents came with a good report. The second, likewise, brought the profits he had earned. The third man did not come until he was sent for. Fearfully he aproached his master and said, "Here it is. I wrapped it up and buried it in the ground because I was afraid."

Why was he afraid? Why are we sometimes afraid of God? Does he not understand our emotions, our fears, our hopes, our dreams? God can read our thoughts. He who knew the stammering of Moses knows also the frustrations that we face today. Throughout the Bible we find the Lord reassuring his people.

"Fear not, Abram," God said to his faithful friend. "I am thy shield, and thy exceeding great reward" (Gen. 15:1). To Isaac, digging a well in the sight of his enemies, God repeated the promises: "I am the God of Abraham thy father: fear not, for I am with thee" (Gen. 26:24). Isaac's son, Jacob, mourned, "Joseph is not, and Simeon is not, and now Benjamin will be taken away. All these things are against me!" Jehovah spoke to Jacob and said, "I am God, the God of thy father: fear not to go down into Egypt" (Gen. 46:3).

At the Red Sea, under the leadership of Moses, the Israelites found they had marched right into a seemingly impossible situation. Uncrossable waters surged before them and the military might of Egypt stormed at their backs. "Fear ye not" was the message of God to Moses in that hour. "Stand still, and see the salvation of the Lord" (Ex.

14:13). The people marveled as the waters rolled back before them.

We serve the same God. He can still make a way for his people, even out of a seemingly impossible situation. Why should we fear the worst of circumstances and enemies? Why should we listen to those who say that God is dead? Our world has been so busy explaining away God, we sometimes feel that it would not know him if it met him face to face.

Facing the Future

How do we face the future? With faith, or with fear? Worry comes in several categories, but one of the most frequent causes of worry is sin. We feel guilty because of the failures in our yesterdays—the words spoken in anger, the deeds that cannot be undone, the influences that cannot be changed. But worry cannot affect a single word or deed, not even a look or an impression. "God requireth that which is past" (Eccl. 3:15).

We worry about what will happen to us in the future. We fear that we will repeat the failures of the past. We easily become so involved with such worries that we do not take time to live the way we should in the present. We do not recognize the importance of today, which is yesterday's future and tomorrow's past. We should rejoice and be glad in the present day, even though sometimes we have to smile through the tears.

God always gives us dividends from difficulties if we trust him. "Thou hast enlarged me when I was in distress" was the joyful testimony of the psalmist who had been through great trials (4:1). We should be careful with today because of its influence upon tomorrow, but carefulness is different from anxiety. When we are told not to worry, however, we take it to mean that we are not to care at all. Relaxation to the point of carelessness becomes a false crutch for our problems. There is a distinction between overanxiety and careful concern. The difference in any given situation can be discovered through prayerful thought. "If Christians spent as much time praying as they do gambling," it has been said, "they would have nothing to grumble about."

We should not worry as we do—we know that. But we should maintain a divinely prompted discontent over things as they are and keep trying to improve them. "I'm worried because I'm not worrying," said an aged minister on one occasion, complaining about his own lethargy.

Too many people worry over trifles and are not concerned enough about the truly important things of life, the spiritual decisions which affect their future in this world and hereafter. But if we have committed our lives and our hopes into the hands of God, we need not allow worry to invade our lives and take up permanent abode!

7

Sanctuary of a Soul

When he had sent the multitudes away, he
went up into a mountain apart to pray: and
when the evening was come, he was there
alone.   Matthew 14:23

In recent years the moving industry has become a major
business in America. We are a nation on the move. Some
people are forced to move by employment transfers and
other reasons; others are quite voluntary. Restlessness often
drives families from one community to another, men from
one job to another. Many people flit from one church to
another. Some change friends often, feeling that it is the
friends they tire of, not recognizing their own instability.
Yet loneliness is also a real problem.

A powerful radio station closes broadcasting each day
with the words, "I bid you a pleasant good night." During
a survey to determine why the station had such a large
listening audience, a woman who held down a very interesting job said that she listened because, out of all the contacts of her day, it was the only time she felt someone was
speaking directly to her. It had become a personal touch
in an impersonal world.

There is real danger that ours might be described as "the
impersonal age." No longer are we a rural people; we have
become an urban nation. Never have men been so close
together, yet so far apart. Cities seem to create loneliness
without solitude. Men now move together to be separated
and get together to be lonely.

A well-known southern statesman of his day, Henry Grady, lived in a great city for a time with his family. There they suffered the loss of a child. "Let's go back home," he said to his wife after the funeral, "where people care when a baby dies." They felt keen loneliness so far away from former friends and neighbors, and the new acquaintances they had made seemed not to care.

There is a vast difference between being just alone and being really lonely. It has been said that "loneliness is when you are forced to be alone against your will; solitude is when you willingly seek to be alone."

Any person who loves beauty finds a thrill in contemplating God's beautiful world. It is not difficult to understand why God made the mountains and streams as he did, the sky and the water, and the leaves of all colors. But how often men have wondered about themselves—why did God make man, knowing how he would turn from him?

God said that he made man in his own image. Is there something in man that reflects the hunger of God for fellowship? Did the loneliness of the universe cause him to want someone to love him voluntarily? Is that why—that he might demonstrate his love by sending his Son Jesus Christ into the world to redeem it?

God knows all things, especially the nature of man. "It is not good that the man should be alone," he said. "I will make him an help meet for him. And [the Lord] brought her unto the man" (Gen. 2:18, 22).

Even at the risk that we would not choose to respond to his love, God willingly gave men freedom of choice. He delights in satisfying the hunger in our hearts as we reach out to him. How often we disappoint him by refusing to come into his presence. We can choose to be entirely alone, or with other people, or alone with him.

Shrouded Seclusion

A wealthy widow complained that she would be utterly alone because she was leaving a house of sixty-eight rooms for a cottage with only twenty-eight, which required only eighteen servants. There are some people who are not aware of anyone else, who isolate themselves in their own little self-interests. But to feel that no one else counts is dangerous, both socially and mentally. When some American explorers found a new tribe of Eskimos and learned to communicate with them, they found that the Eskimos were most amazed by the fact that there were other people at all. In their lonely isolation, they had thought they were the only human beings in the world.

Yet everyone has moments of feeling utterly alone. Some of our loneliness is inevitable. People sometimes say that they are not sure whether it is because they love people or hate themselves, but they do not want to be alone.

There are times when we have to stand alone and serve alone. When Elijah ran away from Ahab and Jezebel and came to a lonely place, he poured out his desolation to God in the words, "I, even I only, am left; and they seek my life, to take it away" (1 Kings 19:10). In solitude of soul, listening for the voice of God, Elijah looked for a show of power. Thunder and lightning, earthquake, wind and fire dazzled Elijah with their display, "but the Lord was not in the fire: and after the fire a still small voice" (1 Kings 19:12). Often God speaks most clearly in silence.

It is interesting to search the Gospels and note the times when Jesus, as man, was alone, and when, as God, he spoke eloquently through silence. His enemies asked him many questions designed to entrap him, and he did not condescend to answer. Before Herod, he refused to say a word; before Pilate, he was strangely silent. The distance between God and these men was so great that it was impossible to communicate.

Even in the midst of loving families loneliness sometimes develops. Martha felt forsaken when her sister did not help her. She complained to Jesus, "Lord, dost thou care that my sister hath left me to serve alone?" (Luke 10:40). There are times when we feel that we carry the whole world on our shoulders and that no one else is really interested.

Then there is the feeling of being unwanted or unappreciated. We have not always fully understood the elder brother of the prodigal son, who obviously felt he was unimportant in his father's sight. He had been working in the back pasture, perhaps. As he came to the house to wash his face and hands, he heard music and asked what was going on.

"Your brother has come back," he was told. "Your father has killed a fatted calf." The older brother ought to have felt good about it; he should have rejoiced with his father whose heart had been broken. But resentment and rebellion arose in him.

"I have been with you all this time," he said to his father, "and you never made any fuss over me. You make a big thing of this boy coming back, but you never did anything for me when I stayed here and worked faithfully all the time." He just went back to the barn, alone.

Strangely enough, parents need to be reminded that there are times when their children feel desperately alone. When they are small, they are often overlooked; they have problems and feel that nobody cares.

Psychologists tell us that, in adolescence more than at any other age, young people want to belong to a group because they feel so desperately alone. Boys have feet as big as men, but they are not old enough to vote and still have to be disciplined by the decisions of others. They feel unaccepted and misunderstood. This contributes to the gang spirit. Young people are eager to do anything as long as they are in the crowd because of their urge not to be left alone.

Families become separated by the demands of business, national security, and for the sake of God's service, and some are left behind. One of our missionaries shared his feelings as he prepared to move across the ocean to serve in another place. "I would like to visit with you longer," he said, "but I must be with my parents. We are leaving them, probably never to see them here again. We are leaving them alone."

The loneliness of advanced age often brings genuine heartbreak. The feeling of being no longer needed, or of being unwanted, is always painful. But people growing older may discover that, although there will be lonely hours, one need not be alone, for the Lord is nearby.

Soul Solitude

Aloneness, when welcomed, frees our minds and spirits for meditation. The best thoughts, usually, come to us in times when we are alone. The greatest poetry and best books are written in periods set apart. The most powerful messages are prepared in undisturbed, undistracted, perhaps midnight hours. Useful inventions are usually dreamed up in the solitude of a single mind, and the deepest prayers prayed in the silences of the soul. In our frustration we are often tempted to do anything just to belong to the group, but there are many important things for which we need to be alone.

However, many people seem to feel a danger in solitude, as if God might really have a chance to get to us if we stopped long enough to hear him speak. In our restlessness, we do not give God an opportunity to have a word with us. We are not willing to pay the price of quietness to experience the reality of God's presence. We may say it is good for our souls to commune with our Maker, but too frequently we go away from church services feeling that we have escaped meeting him.

The Quakers come to their meetinghouse and are silent; nothing is said unless someone feels that the Spirit is leading. When we come to the house of God, quiet periods of worship seem a rarity. If there happens to be a quiet moment, we reach for the bulletin to see what is supposed to be next and wonder who is missing his cue. Silence need not be awkward. It may be awesome, but it can be a blessing.

God meant us to have communion with him and fellowship with one another, but many have difficulty maintaining both fellowships at the same time. Some feel that they come to worship, to be alone with God. Communion with God should enrich and sweeten fellowship between men, but neither can entirely take the place of the other.

Solitude should be sought occasionally. When there is no aloneness of the soul, no time to think long thoughts or pray deep prayers, unnecessary problems and frictions may arise in ourselves and in our relationships with other people.

If circumstances force loneliness upon us, we can seek the communion with the Lord instead of feeling lonely. The apostle Paul used his solitary life profitably in the service of the Lord. Other great saints of God have felt quite alone and yet went on in sweet companionship with God. "The City of Happiness," it has been said, "is located in the State of Mind."

One wrote with true perception, "I needed the quiet, so He drew me aside."

Sympathetic Saviour

Paul described his experience of loneliness in one of his prison epistles, "No man stood with me, but all men forsook me." Then he added, "Notwithstanding the Lord stood with me, and strengthened me" (2 Tim. 4:16-17).

Exiled on Patmos, John described heaven and all that it meant to him in symbolic language, saying that "there was no more sea" (Rev. 21:1). He was separated from all his loved ones by the tossing sea. He felt that when he got to heaven, thank God, there would be no more waters of separation.

Jesus knew what it was to be more completely alone than we will ever be—not only in Gethsemane but on Calvary. As he died, there was one hanging on either side of him, it is true, but they had nothing in common with him. They represented one kind of life and he another. The shadow of complete darkness fell on the cross of Jesus as he was forsaken by God and man.

Therefore, he always understands our loneliness. To those who feel desperately unwanted, Jesus is the friend of friends. To those who feel there is no word of encouragement or comfort for them anywhere, Jesus said, "I will never leave thee, nor forsake thee" (Heb. 13:5).

Our God has always been a God of comfort. He said to Abraham, "Get thee out of thy country, and from thy kindred, and from thy father's house unto a land that I will shew thee: and I will make of thee a great nation, and I will bless thee, and make thy name great; and thou shalt be a blessing" (Gen. 12:1-2). In other words, he was to cut loose from all his human and social contacts. Abraham went out alone, across the uncharted, untracked desert, not knowing where God was leading him. All he had was the promise and the presence of God.

Daniel was taken away from his country and people as a child. Alone in the pagan court of Babylon, the only time he felt close to his own land and people was when he knelt and prayed facing toward Jerusalem. This was against the king's edict, and Daniel was thrown into the lions' den. The next morning the king returned with an anxious question, "Is the God whom thou servest able to deliver thee?"

"My God hath sent his angel," replied Daniel, "and hath shut the lions' mouths, that they have not hurt me" (Dan. 6:22). The question is still asked, and God is still able!

There were three other Hebrews in Babylon who persisted in worshiping their God, in spite of the law that no man should bow down to anyone except the king. These were cast into a furnace, heated seven times hotter than usual. The world will always make it more difficult for the Christian who remains faithful. Yet those who stood and watched heard the pagan ruler's comment: "Lo, I saw four men loose, walking in the midst of the fire, and they have no hurt; and the form of the fourth is like the Son of God" (Dan. 3:25). The Lord did not leave them alone.

Jesus also said that he came to bring release to the captives. Sometimes we become captives by putting ourselves in voluntary confinement such as loneliness and self-pity. God even made a special day for our fellowship with him. "The sabbath was made for man," Jesus said, "and not man for the sabbath" (Mark 2:27).

There is never a time—in the silence of the night, or in the fiery furnace, or in the tests of life—when God ever leaves us alone! There are times, however, when he wants us to be alone, to come apart with him so that we may pray and meditate; he wants us to listen to his words and commune with him. Then we find that even though we are alone, we will never be lonely, for he is with us.

8
Suffering's Cause

The sufferings of this present time are not worthy to be compared with the glory which shall be revealed in us.   Romans 8:18

A minister walked out of a drugstore in a little Kentucky town just in time to overhear the words of a blind couple whom he had noticed when he entered the store. Earlier the sun had been beaming brightly, but all at once clouds had come over and taken away the warmth of sunlight. Although the blind couple could not see, they felt the shadow. The wife said to her husband, "It is darker than it was." Inevitably, there are times in the lives of all of us when it is darker than it was.

Even the spiritually blind of our age, with conditions as they are, say, "It is darker than it was." But when a preacher mentions the sins of yesterday and the problems of today, many people object. They always want to relate the message to someone else rather than to themselves. It is never easy to preach such a message.

In a very old manuscript, we read the complaint of Job as he walked to and fro one sleepless night and rubbed his hands together: "Man that is born of a woman is of few days, and full of trouble" (14:1). He needed comfort that not even his friends could give him. A distressed man said concerning well-meaning friends, "They help, but they don't help much."

Job's friends did not help. They came to him and said, in effect, "Job, we are closer to you than anybody else. We will not tell on you. Evidently this calamity has come upon you because of something you have done. If you will just confess it, you will feel much better and you will not have to suffer any more." They believed that all suffering came as a direct result of sin. Job knew of no sin, secret or otherwise, in his life; and he found no comfort in their words.

Nearly always the first question that comes out of suffering is why. "O God, why did this happen to me?" Why do we have this devastating war? Why do floods come and take off the topsoil? Why does hail destroy our crops? These "whys" fall on the winds that blow through the halls of nowhere. Job's ancient cry is as modern as today. For in the secret places of every soul the questions come: Why sin? Why pain? Why tragedy?

The disciples of Jesus took the same attitude as did Job's friends. They prejudged; they made a snap decision: "Master, who did sin, this man, or his parents, that he was born blind?" (John 9:2).

To them, suffering was always the result of some definite sin on the part of someone. We are much like them in passing judgment on others. We tend to interpret circumstances that we do not understand or comprehend as if someone were at fault; someone has to be to blame—God, society, or the person himself.

Why do the righteous suffer? Instead, may I raise another question, Why should they not suffer, especially since they have something worth suffering for? If men will die for communism, then why should Christians not be willing to suffer for Christ, or even die for him? Is our faith not worth the effort?

Suffering, however, is not entirely random. There are reasons and situations that are basic causes. First, the Christion should recognize that Satan is the supreme adversary

of every child of God, and he plants in every sinful heart
that he controls a feeling of hatred for the man who is
dedicated to the cause of Christ. He obviously is having
his way in many things. Those who seek to witness for
the Lord know that the devil is having much to say in this
world of ours right now.

Jesus warned Simon Peter that the devil would not leave
him alone. "Simon, behold, Satan hath desired to have you,
that he may sift you as wheat" (Luke 22:31). Satan tried
to make Peter deny his Lord, to ruin his testimony so that
it would be worthless. The more completely committed a
Christian is, the more definite opposition he is likely to
encounter. The reason some people do not know there is
a problem is that they are not doing enough for Satan to
worry about.

There are different kinds of suffering, although it is sometimes difficult to classify and impossible to diagnose. The
very real suffering that results from separations between
loved ones is classified as sorrow.

The Bible teaches us, first of all, that there are some con-
sequential sufferings. If men defy the law of gravity or other
natural laws of the Creator, they suffer as a result. If a man
jumps off a cliff, he must expect certain consequences—
unless God performs a miracle to save him.

We may get pushed off the cliff—our sufferings result not
only from our own actions but because of the actions of
other people. A man may say it is nobody's business what
he does. But if his actions recklessly damage others, then
it is somebody's business.

There are also disciplinary sufferings. As an earthly father
disciplines his child, God disciplines his children. "Whom
the Lord loveth he chasteneth, and scourgeth every son
whom he receiveth" (Heb. 12:6). Although we might not

wish to be corrected, he will punish his children who disobey, and leave the mark of his disciplining hand. "No chastening for the present seemeth to be joyous, but grievous: nevertheless afterward it yieldeth the peaceable fruit of righteousness unto them which are exercised thereby" (v. 11).

Some sufferings are designed to be beneficial in other ways. "Master, who did sin, this man, or his parents, that he was born blind?" asked the disciples.

"Neither hath this man sinned, nor his parents," answered Jesus, "but that the works of God may be made manifest in him" (John 9:3).

Jesus did not go to Lazarus immediately when he heard that his friend was sick. Raising Lazarus from the dead was a great manifestation of the works of God.

Then there are substitutionary sufferings. Jeremiah said, out of his knowledge of Israel's sins against God and the sure punishment to come, "Truly this is a grief, and I must bear it" (Jer. 10:19). There are some burdens of our own we must bear, and some that we need to bear for others. But the burden of sin, that terrible blight of our lives, only Jesus could bear, and that on the cross. Paul was referring to this when he expressed his desire, "That I may know him, and the power of his resurrection, and the fellowship of his sufferings" (Phil. 3:10).

How shallow is our knowledge of Christ! Many people feel that all there is to knowing Christ is meeting him at the church altar and accepting his salvation, then leaving him there, outside their everyday lives. That is not crowning him Lord! To know him is to meet him personally at his cross of salvation, and to walk with him in his risen life continuously until he calls us up higher. That may involve suffering.

All kinds of suffering, whatever the pain or whatever the cause, should turn us to God. "Oh, that I knew where I might find him!" Job cried out of his despair, "that I might come even to his seat!" (23:3). In the hurrying around of everyday life we tend to forget the spiritual dimension of life, but when trouble comes we want something beyond the physical and material, and we turn to God, even if only to ask why.

Suffering Because of Sickness

Even though Christians possess eternal life, at present they live in mortal bodies. This body was not made only for one world: "This corruptible must put on incorruption, and this mortal must put on immortality. . . . Then shall be brought to pass the saying that is written, Death is swallowed up in victory" (1 Cor. 15:53-54). Living in this mortal body, we still have its mortal problems, even though we are eternity-bound.

This body suffers from injury and disease. Death is terrible, but sometimes living seems worse than death for the believer when the body is wracked with pain or helplessly disabled.

"The world is full of trouble," said Helen Keller, and we would expect her to say that, but not to go on and say, "and the world is full of ways that you can overcome trouble." This, many of us have not found. We have stopped far short of her faith and optimism.

Walt Whitman called suffering "the great comradeship." "It is the unseen order," said William James. Suffering is universal. Everyone suffers in some way, sometimes with almost unbearable physical or mental pain. Often suffering makes men brothers in the bonds of sympathy.

An elderly Christian lady had been in the hospital for

some time and, because of her advanced years, there seemed to be no healing. She would probably be bedfast the rest of her life. Her mind was quite alert as she was put into the ambulance to go to a convalescent home.

"May I ask a favor?" she said to the attendants. "It isn't far out of the way to go by my church," she explained. "I just wondered if you would mind. You know," she added wistfully, "it just might be the last time I'll ever see it."

The ambulance driver pulled up in front of the church building and let her take as much time as she liked. She told them how she loved her church and thanked them for allowing her to have a look at it. One of these men is active in church today because, as he said, "I never knew what the church could mean before. Not until I saw how much it meant to one who might never again be able to go inside its doors."

Sometimes suffering can make a man feel his need of the church. God never wills suffering for us. He will always make it "work together for good to them that love God" (Rom. 8:28).

Concerning a contemporary composer whom he knew well, Beethoven once remarked, "I'm afraid he will never make a great musician. He was never flogged enough as a boy." A man who has not suffered cannot sympathize with others; he cannot stir their souls with music because he has never really been touched. Even after deafness struck, Beethoven struggled on through suffering and contributed much to the music world.

The writer to the Hebrews has given us a very comforting verse which says, "We have not an high priest which cannot be touched with the feeling of our infirmities" (4:15). Not only did the Lord Jesus weep one day by the tomb of Lazarus, he weeps with us also. He not only suffered for us on Golgotha, he suffers with us today. If we can only realize the presence of God and his sympathy in the midst of our suffering, it makes all the difference! Indeed, suffering may serve to make us bitter or better.

Suffering Because of Slight

There is much suffering because of slight, estrangement, and hurt feelings. It is a suffering more prevalent than is realized. Yet to strengthen ourselves, it would be wise to admit that feeling hurt is to invite the repetition of such hurt. On the other hand, we often dismiss the imaginary hurts of others, almost rudely, although they are very painful to the one who suffers them. In fact, it is more difficult to deal with the shadows of imagination than with the realities of pain.

Self-pity flowers rapidly out of slights. It is difficult to handle and easily develops into a martyr complex that is dangerously neurotic. Those who try to make their lives count for Christ expose themselves to slight and ridicule. One man expressed the hindering power of ridicule: "I'd rather be jailed than to be laughed at." Sometimes Christians feel it would be easier to face the threat of real persecution than the jibes of their associates.

D. L. Moody was frequently criticized because he used incorrect grammar. It hurt him, but he tried to take it as constructive criticism. He was a shoe salesman when God laid it upon his heart to be a witness for him. He would never be ordained, but remained a lay preacher to the day of his death. "It's true that I haven't had the benefits of formal education," he replied to those who criticized him. "I haven't had the chances some people have. God being my helper, I am trying to do the best I can with what I have."

Are we doing the best we can with what we have? There

are many people who will not serve the Lord because they are afraid of criticism. Thereby many who would not think of slighting their fellowman are slighting God.

Suffering Because of Sin

When the Jews demanded that Pilate release Barabbas instead of Jesus, he asked, "Why, what evil hath he done? . . . I am innocent of the blood of this just person" (Matt. 27:23-24). This Roman governor had heard the teachings of the rabbis and he knew the thoughts of the Hebrew people. He had the same problem concerning suffering, and, as a judge, a question concerning punishment. He could find no evidence of guilt. This man who was absolutely guiltless, who had no sin, was nevertheless condemned to suffer the most cruel punishment men could devise. He suffered as no other man ever suffered in being forsaken also by God.

Sin brings suffering—mankind cannot doubt that fact. The heaviest burden any man bears is the load of unconfessed guilt, whether he is conscious of it or not. "Therefore to him that knoweth to do good," the Bible declares, "and doeth it not, to him it is sin" (James 4:17). An Old Testament maxim says, "The wicked flee when no man pursueth" (Prov. 28:1). They know in their hearts that they are guilty, and they feel that everybody is talking about them and condemning them.

In his song about two kinds of men, the psalmist summarized, "Therefore the ungodly shall not stand in the judgment, nor sinners in the congregation of the righteous. For the Lord knoweth the way of the righteous: but the way of the ungodly shall perish" (Psalm 1:5-6).

In ancient days it was the custom for kings to go into the prisons at certain times and grant pardons to whomever they would. Frederick the Great went into one prison and walked from cell to cell, asking each man about his guilt. "I am innocent!" they all claimed.

Finally he came to one who surprised him by confessing, "I am guilty. I deserve everything I have received in the way of punishment."

The ruler immediately called the guard. "Let this man go free," he commanded.

We can never get out of the prison of sin until we come before God with our guilt and confess it. We cannot escape the results of our sin which may cause us grief and sorrow, but we can avoid the suffering of guilt when we lay down that burden by confession. We can never conquer sin; it is a cancer which must be removed by God's surgery.

Jesus came to set the captives free, even those bound by strong chains of sin and guilt. He came to reconcile us with our Father from whom we have been separated by sin. Whatever separates us from God—sin, pain or suffering, coldness of heart—it need not be. God stands with open arms to forgive and receive and comfort all who come to him. He has promised that he will wipe away all tears from our eyes, and suffering will be no more.

9
Sorrow

Blessed be God, even the Father of our Lord
Jesus Christ, the Father of mercies, and the
God of all comfort; who comforteth us in all
our tribulation, that we may be able to com-
fort them which are in any trouble, by the
comfort wherewith we ourselves are com-
forted of God. 2 Corinthians 1:3-4

An ancient king brought together a great number of
scholars to write a history of mankind. They compiled many
thick books, but in the pressure of his duties the king did
not have time to read them. Finally, in the sunset years of
his life, he brought the same men to his palace and commissioned them to make a summary of their history for him.
One of the group spoke up. "Sire, I can do that right now
in three statements," he said. "Man was born, he suffered,
he died. That is the history of all mankind."

We know that death is inevitable, not only for ourselves,
but also for our loved ones. Even though the intellect may
be prepared, the heart always rebels, because death is the
most completely shattering experience suffered by the human personality. "Never a morning wore to evening," wrote
Tennyson, "but some heart did break."

How do we react to the heartbreak of sorrow? Some people, seemingly on the brink of despair, bow their heads and
say, "Why, O God? Why?" Sometimes it is hard to tell
whether the words are profanity or prayer. Sorrow is not
like an automatic escalator that, once you step on the lower

step, will carry you up to new heights with God. This can be so, but sometimes nothing could be farther from the truth. The experience of sorrow is more like the automatic elevator, where you have to decide the direction you want to go and push the button. It can take you either up or down. There are some who go through the valley of the shadow of death and stand higher than ever before in the presence of God, but not all.

The philosophers of this world have little to offer on the subject of death, except that it is an inevitable fact. "There is a fullness of time when all men must go," wrote Thomas Jefferson. A common maxim says, with sharp poignancy, "The old must die; the young may die." In an attempt at wit, it has been said, "You can't get out of this life alive." No, we can't—but he who believes in Christ shall never truly die! Everyone has an interest in death, whether he admits it or not. Consciously or unconsciously, men cannot live without wondering about the other end of life.

The only place we can find the answers to our questions about death is in God's Word. The great statements and promises of the Bible tell us many things we could not otherwise know. "It is appointed unto men once to die," the Bible declares, "but after this the judgment" (Heb. 9:27). God's word on the subject adds the idea that after this life there must be an accounting.

In the Bible, emphasis is placed upon the fact that God himself is talking to us, as in the words of Jesus Christ: "Let not your heart be troubled: ye believe in God, believe also in me. In my Father's house are many mansions: if it were not so, I would have told you. I go to prepare a place for you" (John 14:1-2). If we accept the sweet assurance of these words, we can comfort ourselves in the words of the psalmist: "The Lord is my shepherd; I shall not want. . . .

Yea, though I walk through the valley of the shadow of death, I will fear no evil: for thou art with me. . . . Surely goodness and mercy shall follow me all the days of my life: and I will dwell in the house of the Lord for ever" (Psalm 23:1-6).

A farmer, after completing a new barn, put up a big lightning rod. The weather that day was so beautiful it seemed to mock such a precaution, but he did not let it deceive him. He knew that inevitably the storms would come. In sunshine he was preparing for the storms.

It always helps to be prepared. It is too late to talk about insurance when the house is on fire. When life tumbles in, what then? The best time to make provision for the difficult hours is before they arrive, before you feel numb and helpless. In the sunrise of a man's life, and even more in the noontime, it is important for him to realize that there are going to be sunset hours ahead.

Many of the funerals I conduct are for people who have no connection at all with a church. Sometimes strangers come to me afterwards and say, "Preacher, you'll never know what your help has meant to us." Others walk away without a word, as if they felt God had dealt them a miserable blow and they wanted nothing to do with him. One man stood by a graveside and said, "Preacher, you will never again preach in this city without my coming to hear you." And it was true—after that experience he became a faithful member. The Master Teacher of the universe uses all of the experiences of our lives, including loss and sorrow, to lead us to himself.

A florist's truck that preceded us to the cemetery one day had a sign on it which said, "Crosses and wreaths made to order." This reflects the nature of man's response to any difficulty in life. We have something to say about the size and shape of our burdens, and how we attempt to carry them. When an impossible situation crashes down upon our lives, either we can try to shoulder it by ourselves, or we can admit that it is too big for us to handle and take it to the Lord. He is always waiting to help us, whatever the load.

Is Sorrow Selfish?

Sometimes, however, we hug our burden of grief and do not allow the Lord to lift it from us with his comfort. Thus our sorrow tends to be selfish as we think only of our own grief and loss.

For those we love, we want the best. Parents are willing to work their hands to the bone for their children. Whether the child appreciates it or not matters little as far as the parent is concerned. Love overcomes all things. We would voluntarily take the place of our child on a sickbed or an operating table or at the cemetery, if we could.

Therefore, in the quiet sanctuary of our souls, we need to ask ourselves, in our sorrow, if we weep for them or for ourselves. Mostly, we weep for our unbearable loneliness. We weep because we are separated, because we are hurt. We weep as we make the necessary adjustments in life. All of this is inevitable. "There is no home without its hush," goes a Spanish proverb. In the Bible, we are not told not to weep, only that as Christians we should "sorrow not, even as others which have no hope" (1 Thess. 4:13).

Jesus said repeatedly, "Let not your heart be troubled!" The best way to bring sorrow into perspective is to raise a practical question. Would we, if we could, bring our loved ones back from heaven to this earth? Would we do it for their sake, or for our own? Do we not believe that being in heaven is an existence far more wonderful than we can imagine?

"Loose him, and let him go" Jesus said to the friends of Lazarus (John 11:44). Those of us who have lost a loved one need to heed his admonition. It is, of course, the most difficult thing in all the world—may I say it tenderly—for us to let them go. "Lord, if thou hadst been here," Martha reproved Jesus, "my brother had not died" (John 11:21).

"Thy brother shall rise again," Jesus told her. "Whosoever liveth and believeth in me shall never die. Believest thou this?" (John 11:23, 26).

To the sisters, his words held little meaning. At that moment the future seemed so unimportant, the present so pressing. They were concerned for the moment rather than with eternity.

At the grave of Lazarus, we are told, Jesus wept. He wept out of sympathy with the sorrow of his friends, even when he knew that in a moment Lazarus would live again.

Reaction often needs to be guided in the time of shock, but death is not a Pollyanna affair. It is most often life's deepest hurt. "Whatever you do," said one who came to the door when a pastor visited a home where there had been the loss of a loved one, "don't sympathize with her."

"Why not?" he asked. That was the reason he had come. Those who are strong in the Lord are those who have followed the Lord's example. Weeping, yes; grief, yes; peace, yes!

Jesus also prayed. You say, "I come to a time when I can't pray." Then I ask you, What is prayer to you? Is it just a recital of words? Or is it pouring out to God the things that lie heavy on our hearts? That is prayer at its best—when life is at its worst. Jesus prayed even on the cross.

If eternity is already a reality in our hearts and minds, we will catch a glimpse of triumph even in the hour of death. "He is near the land of the dying," whispered those by the bedside of an old Scottish preacher. Overhearing them, he answered, "Nay! I'm now in the land of the dying; I am near the land of the living!"

Separation

Shakespeare captured the imagination of the young when he said, "Parting is such sweet sorrow." Separation is always sad between those who love, whether it lasts for a day or for an indefinite time.When children go away to play for an hour or so, there is a loneliness. When they go off to college, there is separation. Certain adjustments are necessary. When they go beyond this life, the separation seems much longer and more definite, and always it comes sooner than we think.

Not only do we have to let them go, but we too die a little bit, a day at a time. Every time I have left a pastorate, I died a little in the separation. We cannot turn loose of those whom we love without some feeling akin to sorrow in our hearts.

The aged apostle John, who wrote of himself as "the disciple whom Jesus loved," was exiled to the lonely island of Patmos. There God gave him a great vision of heaven. We, like John, could have more vision if we were in the spirit on the Lord's Day.

As John stood on the lonesome beach and looked across the sea toward the mainland, he thought of the friends and fellow workers he loved over there in Asia Minor, from whom he was separated. He wept for himself as well as for his friends across the waves. He dreamed of the time when there would be no separation: "I saw a new heaven and a new earth: for the first heaven and the first earth were passed away; and there was no more sea" (Rev. 21:1). The greatest suffering John was experiencing was that of separation, and to him the sea was a symbol of that separation. "One of these days," he comforted himself, "this separating sea will be removed and I'll be with the Lord and with all those I love."

"God shall wipe away all tears from their eyes," John wrote in a paean of joy at the prospect. "There shall be no more death, neither sorrow, nor crying, neither shall there be any more pain: for the former things are passed away" (Rev. 21:4).

Each time one goes to the silent city and hears repeated these precious promises, we are caused to think more of our Christian faith than ever before. Our Lord is a sustaining help in the great crises of life and death. Even for separation he has the great cure, that it is only temporary, and in the meantime we should not think of the grave but of the glory.

"When you see in the headlines that I am dead," D. L. Moody once said, "don't you believe it! I'll be alive as never before!"

"O death, where is thy sting?" exclaimed Paul, rising to the very heights of inspiration in his chapter on resurrection. "O grave, where is thy victory?" (1 Cor. 15:55). It is possible to take the sting out of a bee. It is possible to take the poison sac from a snake. But is it possible to remove from death its deadly sting? Paul insisted that although death must come, God has taken the sting out of it.

In a section in his life of Abraham Lincoln called "The Prairie Years," Carl Sandburg said that the settlers' hands were like giant oaks. They buried their loved ones with their own hands and shovels, for there were no neighbors near when fever struck them down.

The only thing that kept the survivors going was their faith. When the preacher came to the community, they

would gather and "wash their souls in revival." Some of the
sting was removed when they could sing,

> There's a land that is fairer than day,
> And by faith we can see it afar.

Even more than that, our faith can anticipate, as Fanny
Crosby, the blind hymn writer who gave us so many songs
that touch our hearts, expressed it:

> Some day the silver cord will break,
> And I no more as now shall sing;
> But O, the joy when I shall wake
> Within the palace of the King!
>
> And I shall see him face to face,
> And tell the story—Sav'd by grace!

When you have a headache, probably a doctor can help
you, or when you have a toothache, a dentist can help. But
when you have a heartache, only the Great Physician can
help! Jesus did not say that we should escape death, but he
did say that he would remove the sting of it.

Sometimes, in their last moments, people get what seems
to be a glimpse of the beyond and find strength to express
it in words. "If this is death," said Robert Louis Stevenson,
a great writer who was familiar with the hard hand of pain,
"it is easy." Thomas Edison, in the last moments of his life,
said that he did not expect death to be this way: "It is
beautiful over there." And Tennyson said, "If this is death,
life is the dull side of it."

Here, when we have lost a loved one, we say, "He is
gone." In Africa the believers say, "He has arrived!"

A man who had just lost his father thanked his pastor for
standing by and for giving the memorial message by saying, "You have made an unbearable day . . . bearable."

It is the grace of Jesus that makes all things bearable! The best adjustment for our sorrow and loss because of the separation of death is to realize that the Saviour bears it with us. He was indeed "a man of sorrows and acquainted with grief" (Isa. 53:3). Now he is our "high priest . . . touched with the feeling of our infirmities" (Heb. 4:15).

10
Shackles

He said unto me, My grace is sufficient for thee: for my strength is made perfect in weakness. Most gladly therefore will I rather glory in my infirmities, that the power of Christ may rest upon me. 2 Corinthians 12:9

In the prime of life, an active man became crippled by polio. Knowing he might be confined to his bed indefinitely, and having a secret desire to write, he started a biography that had always been dear to his heart. He loved the sea and the people of the sea, and had a special interest in John Paul Jones. Hopefully he sent off his manuscript to a movie studio. The rejection slip, he declared later, seemed the most bitter defeat of his life.

This man thought his usefulness was over, but God had other plans. Franklin Delano Roosevelt did not become a writer but the leader of a nation during very difficult times. After his death, his wife was asked if she thought he would have become president if he had not had polio. "Yes," she replied, "but a president of a different kind."

Nearly every man has some sort of handicap. Almost everyone has limitations—whether he wants to admit it or not, whether he even recognizes it or not. The important thing is how we handle our handicaps. The problems are greatly multiplied when the handicap controls us.

As individuals come to know one another better, as good friends share lovingly with one another secrets of life and heart, each recognizes in the other certain strengths and strange weaknesses. Many a person has pulled himself to a higher plane of living in spite of shackles. To know the handicaps of another does not create pity, but rather stronger love, understanding, and admiration if they have been surmounted.

One of the crucial hours in any life is when a man faces up to the shackles which handicap him—mentally, physically, or psychologically. By nature we resent the things which hold us down. To face them and admit our limitations is a sign of maturity. Growth lies in accepting the things which cannot be changed and trying to better that which can be changed.

Sometimes sudden disaster overtakes a family, a community, or a nation. Natural calamities that we do not understand we label "acts of God." Untold deaths and unnumbered miseries result from floods, hurricanes, tornados. There are also man-made tragedies—war, attack, accident. When one is injured and restricted by such occurrences, it is difficult to rise above the handicap. It is very easy to allow oneself to be shackled by bitterness and self-pity.

It always seems that our own difficulty is the worst. Yet with many disabilities comes added sensitivity in other fields. What worse thing could happen to a musician than to become deaf? Yet Beethoven carried on his music and wrote compositions of great strength and depth, perhaps even better than those written when he could hear. John Milton, in spite of his blindness, gave us some of the most awesome poetry in the world. It is human to see first the somber things in our own circumstances, but if we look around at others, we see that no man seems to escape difficulties.

Many men in all ages have made fine contributions to mankind and have revealed true greatness only after suf-

fering and tragedy. The African explorer Stanley, buried
with honor in Westminster Abbey among the great men of
the British Empire, spent his early years in an almshouse.
It was always a crushing thing to him, never knowing his
mother's name. He always felt a haunting loneliness at the
holiday season particularly, because he felt he belonged to
nobody. Nevertheless, he gave himself to the world in service.

Some people take the attitude of trying to ignore the
handicaps and problems of the world. Until a certain problem affects us personally, we find no reason to search God's
Word for answers to the sorrows and problems of life. Although we may not have shackles at the moment, we never
know when personal tragedy will strike us. The time will
come when we need to be sure that our faith is fixed in God,
that our anchor holds securely.

Even in the more pleasant pastures of life we need the
promises of God. But when difficulties come, we cling to
such comforting words as, "Fear thou not; for I am with
thee: be not dismayed; for I am thy God: I will strengthen
thee; yea, I will help thee; yea, I will uphold thee with the
right hand of my righteousness" (Isa. 41:10).

Handling Handicaps

One of the best examples of overcoming handicaps in the
Old Testament was Joseph, the great-grandson of Abraham.

As a youth, Joseph suffered because of jealousy. The first
son of Jacob's beloved wife, Rachel, Joseph was so highly
favored by his father that his ten brothers resented him
greatly. When they found an opportunity to get rid of him,
they sold him into slavery and let their father think he was
dead.

In Egypt, Joseph's master soon learned to value the honest

and intelligent young man, quickly promoting him to the position of manager of the entire household. As handsome as he was capable, Joseph caught the eye of his master's wife, but when he rejected her, she accused him to her husband, and Joseph was thrown into prison. From the very beginning, the devil has practiced the art of making smoke without fire in his warfare against God's people. Few men have suffered as many setbacks as Joseph—envy, hatred, slander. All handicaps are not physical.

Even in prison, Joseph was outstanding for his wisdom and faithfulness, but when he found opportunity to appeal his case to the Pharaoh, the man who promised to plead for him forgot all about Joseph.

"Who knoweth whether thou art come to the kingdom for such a time as this?" was the question asked Queen Esther by her uncle (Esther 4:14). The question also applied to Joseph. In the great drama of history he had a part to play. Did God cause all the difficulties he suffered? God certainly did not cause Joseph's brothers to sin. He would have used some other method of getting Joseph to Egypt if the sons of Jacob had not acted against their brother in wicked jealousy.

Back in the Promised Land, godly Jacob lamented and complained, half mumbling to himself, "Joseph is not, and Simeon is not, and ye will take Benjamin away." Then he added this pathetic cry: "All these things are against me" (Gen. 42:36). He felt it bitterly and it seemed so true.

The day finally came when Joseph's brothers stood before him, the unrecognized man who was premier of Egypt, and bowed low as in his childhood dream. Their very lives were in his hand, and they pled for mercy. Be sure that those you judge will one day judge you!

Joseph did not permit himself to be eaten up by resentment of the wrong they had done him. Only a man who suffered unjustly without self-pity could have shown such gracious forgiveness as Joseph. Only a man who had endured prison and conquered the imprisonment of self, only a man who had waited long yet trusted God could learn such mercy. "But as for you," Joseph said at the loving reunion with his brothers, "ye thought evil against me; but God meant it unto good, to bring to pass, as it is this day, to save much people alive" (Gen. 50:20).

Let the world do its worst—no matter how the ungodly men intend evil, God can always turn circumstances to glorify his name. It takes a steady hand to carry a full cup across the room; when the cup is half empty it is no problem. Joseph was meant to carry the responsibility of life and death for millions of people, and it took a man with steady hands and a pure heart before God. His handicaps, his shackles, had provided a testing and training program.

Testimony of Paul

In the New Testament the apostle Paul knew what it was to suffer, to be scorned, to be persecuted, but he by no means developed a martyr complex. He recognized that the maximum of God's grace and strength was available for all of his insufficiencies and weaknesses. "I know how to live humbly," he said. "I also know how to live in prosperity" (Phil. 4:12, Moffatt).

Evidently Paul felt that his greatest handicap was physical. He referred to it only as his "thorn in the flesh." He prayed to God three times for it to be removed. Whether this was a literal or a figurative thing, we cannot be entirely sure. Through the years many have guessed about it: some think it was eye trouble, others that it was epilepsy. One thing we can know—it was not a wrong attitude, for he had already overcome that. If it were your problem or mine, the world would probably know all about it without having to guess. Paul maintained dignity in his suffering. The nature of his thorn in the flesh remains unknown to us; whether or not it was known to his contemporaries we cannot be sure.

We are told the really important thing about it, however. To Paul's earnest prayers, God said no. Paul must have been puzzled. Why? he must have wondered. But we cannot presume to know the mind of God, and as it was very important to Paul, he asked again. The second time God said no. When he asked the third time, God told him that he did not choose to take it away, but that he would give Paul the strength and the grace to live with it and to do his work in spite of it.

"My grace is sufficient for thee," was God's effective answer to Paul's prayers. "I will not do what you ask, but I will take care of your need." This is what God says to us, also, many times.

One of the great antislavery leaders in England was a man named Wilberforce. On his grave is the epitaph, "Friend of the friendless and penniless." What greater tribute could a man have?

"When I saw him climb up on the box to speak on slavery," wrote Boswell, "I thought he was not as big as a shrimp. But then I heard him speak, and he became as big as a whale." Wilberforce had the strength of a crusader. Although much of the time he had to live on medicines, until he dared not take any more, he endured tremendous suffering in order that his mind might be clear to speak the message that was burning inside him.

Sometimes we may suffer in order that we might know better the sufferings of Christ. Paul got hold of more theology and more religion than we dare desire to know when he said, "That I may know him, and the power of his resurrection." I can go that far, but Paul went on to say, "and the fellowship of his sufferings" (Phil. 3:10).

What were his sufferings? In Gethsemane, Jesus prayed about the cross which loomed before him, calling it a bitter cup of which he must drink. The first time he prayed, God did not answer; there was only stillness. He prayed the second time—oh, the pathos of it when he said, "O my Father, if this cup may not pass away from me, except I drink it, thy will be done" (Matt. 26:42). God gave no other sense of direction; no other plan was offered. Jesus, in complete submission of God's will, went on to the cross.

The suffering of the cross exceeded anything we can possibly imagine. Not the physical suffering itself—many men have had comparable pain. He gave himself up to all the handicaps of the world and suffered all the agony of its sin and hatred—cruel pain indeed to one who was loving and sinless. He suffered the blackness of death and hell through separation from God—he who had been one with him since eternity.

Our world is not upheld by the strength of a Greek Atlas; it has been pulled together by the weakness of a Jew on a cross. Superhuman strength could not save us, only arms stretched out in obedience and superhuman love.

Experience of Today

If we counted out all the men who have suffered, we would lose most of the best contributions made to this world economically, politically, benevolently, religiously. Many great sufferers have built enduring monuments through sensitivity of spirit and greatness of heart as they have gone through life, especially those who have been in tune with God. This makes a difference. They threw off their shackles!

One man who worked in a boiler room developed tuberculosis and went out to the West Coast for his health, a seriously ill man. Who would be willing to say it is good to be sick? Yet Luther Burbank made a very great contribution to the world. "Every weed can become a flower" was his motto.

Louis Pasteur at the age of forty-six suffered a stroke. After that he had to drag himself back into his laboratory painfully and force himself through grueling hours over his microscope to continue his research. We remember his name and his contribution, but we rarely think of his handicaps.

Many thousands have enjoyed the delightful book *Life with Father*. So crippled with arthritis was the author, Clarence Day. that his pencil had to be taped to his hand. Yet he made the world laugh! We rarely remember the pain the man endured as we rejoice that he gave us something light and wonderful.

If some decisive handicap threatens our bodies or homes, then what shall we do? When tragedy comes, we face a time of examination not only in ourselves but in the eyes of others. Every man has his troubles, but happiness is something he has to create! When failures catch up with us, or tragedy attacks, we are offered either dead-end streets or open doors.

The greatest violinist of his day, Ole Bull was playing a concert in Paris when the A-string of his violin snapped. He could have smashed his instrument in a fit of temper and walked off the stage. Or, he might have asked for another violin, or waited for intermission. Instead, he demonstrated his virtuosity by playing the rest of the concert on just three strings. Few people go through life with only first choices. We have only one life to live, one testimony to give, and we have to play out our concert on the strings that are left—or give up in sour defeat.

"Morale," it has been said, "is when your hands and feet keep on working when your head says it can't be done."

Jesus prayed, "If there is any other way." That was the turning point. If there had been no cross, we would have no Saviour. Christ reconciled the world to God by submission to the worst that men could do to him. God said, "My strength is made perfect in weakness."

The promise given to Paul was not a new principle. It had been exemplified already in his Lord. "Most gladly therefore will I rather glory in my infirmities, that the power of Christ may rest upon me" (2 Cor. 12:9).

11
The Lengthening Shadows

They that wait upon the Lord shall renew their strength; they shall mount up with wings as eagles; they shall run, and not be weary, they shall walk, and not faint.

Isaiah 40:31

In every life there comes a time when it is necessary to sit down to somber thoughts that one had rather not face. Sometimes a man enjoys his work so much that he does not notice the clock, but eventually he has to notice the calendar. A person may get so wrapped up in his job that he spins like a top, but if the spin alone holds him up, when it runs down, he falls over. Many men, for instance, look forward to retirement, but when they get there find only emptiness.

As we face advancing years, we wish we could declare a truce with time. It is very easy, on our modern highways in comfortable automobiles, to think we are driving sixty miles an hour when we are really moving eighty. What is true there is often true physically. It is not hard to arrive at the age of sixty-five while we are still "thinking forty." We move from one age to another with increasing velocity, and it is difficult for us to recognize the advancing years until something happens to make us face them.

What is old age? At one time the ages of mankind were thought of in three main divisions; now we recognize more than twice that many: infancy, childhood, adolescence, early adulthood, middle age, later maturity, and advanced age, which is reached at about eighty. The span of life has increased greatly in the last century. When Gladstone was writing his history of England and mentioned William Pitt, he said that the great man died of old age—at forty-six!

Actually, our concept of age is psychological. The effects of age vary with personality, circumstances, and physical condition. As we grow older, we are naturally inclined to judge those our own age to be just a little bit older than we are. The age measurement that most of us use, it is said, is the span of ten years. We consider others a different age from ourselves if they are at least ten years older or younger than we are.

The Bible recognizes the problems of age and its insecurity. "Cast me not off in the time of old age," prayed the psalmist. "Forsake me not when my strength faileth" (71:9).

The truth of the matter is, however, that it is not really old age itself that causes the difficulty, but rather the fear of old age. The middle-aged tend to look at the future with apprehension. There are both physical and psychological reasons for this. Of course, old age has its special problems, its special diseases. But there are certain childhood diseases also; every age of life has its peculiar ailments and difficulties.

When we really arrive at an advanced age, we do not think so much about it. Most people eighty or over tell their age with pride and perhaps even add advice about how to live so long. But in middle age there is the dread of getting old, a restlessness concerning what to do about life. Frequently there is a feeling of failure and regret for the passing of opportunities. This is especially true of parents when the children are gone and the home becomes empty again.

A bridal party was over and the father of the bride was

watching his wife put aside some of the things for their daughter to pick up when she came back after her honeymoon. With tears in her eyes, the mother said, "What will I do now?" Her husband was a wise man when he said to her, "Why don't we try marriage?"

It is easy to get so busy, so involved in business, community, and home duties, that we cease to live each day as if it were precious in itself. Many people look on the future as if it were filled with more threat than promise. The difficulty arises when we feel that life is closing in, that we have come to a dead end. Ours is a culture of youth, perhaps to our great impoverishment, if we neglect the wisdom and balance of age. "A civilization is known" said one great man, "by how it treats its old people."

Fatalist

Is old age valuable or worthless? Many seem to think that it is a useless burden. We know the difference between a pessimist and an optimist, but more deadly than these is the fatalist. In old age the fatalist seems to see nothing good in life, nothing left in life. This is never true. Such an attitude destroys the joy of any age or of any experience in life. Once it completely destroyed a testimony service. One man mentioned the prospect of rest after death. The fatalist replied bitterly, "With my luck, the next morning would be the resurrection!" A fatalist is not just a lonely person who has fears but one who prefers them.

A man with prematurely gray hair received a lot of teasing about it. "Don't you mind your hair being gray?" his friends would ask in loving sport. "No, I don't mind," he would answer with a laugh. "If it wasn't gray, I might not have any at all!"

This man was a delightful exception. The words of Charles

Lamb, "Our spirits grow grey before our hair," are more true of most people.

There are always some good things around us; there is some kind of opportunity in every age and in every hour that God gives us. There are times, of course, when we feel that we are useless; this is true with every person who ever lived. But it does not mean that God has ever let anyone outlive his usefulness.

The psalmist had a sense of purpose in his old age. "Now also when I am old and grayheaded," he prayed, "O God, forsake me not; until I have shewed thy strength unto this generation, and thy power to every one that is to come" (71:18).

"There is no reason for me to linger longer," many say. But God disagrees. He would not leave you here without definite purpose. In finding out and living out that purpose, the elderly can find great joy and satisfaction. Unfortunately, the longer one lives and the more one learns, the more fears he is apt to acquire.

One grand old minister of South Carolina, S. L. Morgan, went back to a former pastorate to preach when he was eighty-eight years old. His sermon subject was on conquering life's three greatest fears. The first, he said, was fear of old age. Who could speak on that more eloquently than he? Yet at home he had a wife who had been an invalid for many years. The second fear the old preacher mentioned was the fear of death; and the third, fear of things worse than death.

Many of us have seen these fears in ourselves and in others. Although we cannot understand all the providences of God or the twistings of sin, we cannot dump all the things that happen to us at the feet of God and blame him. Some experiences naturally come our way in the course of living.

One really never grows old until his ideas harden, not just when his arteries harden. The fatalistic view should never be characteristic of one who claims to be a Christian. God's ideal is set forth in the Old Testament: "Thine age shall be clearer than the noonday; thou shalt shine forth, thou shalt be as the morning" (Job 11:17).

Faith

Someone has written that old age is a great work of art. I disagree, though that is a beautiful sentiment. Growing old gracefully is a work of faith! As the ties of vigor and usefulness and companionship loosen, the ties of faith must strengthen to hold the spirit securely.

The plantings of a lifetime show their fruit in old age. You may see people living side by side who show great differences in the fruits of their lives and the climates of their hearts as they face advancing years. The devil has no happy old people. The pleasures of worldliness and sin pall and leave a great emptiness. There is nothing so pathetic as a miserable old man who has cursed God with his life and has come to the time when he fearfully faces meeting him. There is nothing such people can think about with real happiness, nothing they can remember with peace, no reward they can anticipate with joy.

Faith shapes beautiful elderly people. Just as an old church seems beautiful, having withstood the storms of time, inside and out, and the devil in the midst, so is the saint of God beautiful who has stood faithful through the years. His very presence among us gives us a benediction and a blessing.

"Be thou my strong habitation, whereunto I may continually resort," prayed a godly man in his old age. "Thou hast given commandment to save me; for thou art my rock and my fortress" (Psalm 71:3). This revealed his desire for security and peace. The Lord has given special promises for the elderly who trust in him. "Even to your old age I am he; and even to hoar hairs will I carry you: I have made, and I will bear; even I will carry, and will deliver you" (Isa. 46:4).

The testimony of an aged person is convincing. When such a man or woman declares that "it pays to serve Jesus, it pays every day," the words are backed up by real proof. "The hoary head is a crown of glory," says the Bible, "if it be found in the way of righteousness" (Prov. 16:31).

The presence of the aged among us seems to bring out tender instincts in human nature, just as does the presence of children. This is right and Christian. In some pagan countries, where a loving God is not glorified, it is possible for helpless old people to be turned over to medical researchers for experimental purposes. Dare to touch one for whom Christ died? Their very presence should bring refreshing and loving thoughts of their tender touch in other years. Old age has a special beauty all its own in those who have the spirit of agelessness. One gracious lady responded to the question of a child about her age by saying, "I'm not really old, but I have been young a very long time."

The added years of old age give us a chance to correct some of our mistakes. King Manasseh of Judah reigned for fifty-five years, and for most of that time led his people in wickedness and idolatry. But after the chastening experience of being taken to Babylon in chains, he repented and came back a different man. He tried to undo some of the damage he had done and to live for the Lord like his godly father Hezekiah. "When he was in affliction," the record says, "he besought the Lord his God, and humbled himself greatly before the God of his fathers, . . . And he repaired the altar of the Lord, . . . and commanded Judah to serve the Lord God of Israel" (2 Chron. 33:12-16).

King David, in his later years, wanted to build the house of God. The prophet Nathan came to him with God's answer: "Thus saith the Lord, Thou shalt not build me an house to dwell in (1 Chron. 17:4). Then after giving David many other wonderful promises, the Lord added concerning Solomon, "He shall build me an house, and I will stablish his throne for ever" (v. 12). The years of old age give us a chance to live again in our children, in a sense. Did David mind so much when he had God's promise that his son would build the temple of his dreams?

In the last century, when Lottie Moon first came home and challenged other women to join her on the mission field, one young woman wanted to answer that call. But in the South, those reconstruction days were very difficult, and there was no money for education or for sending her overseas. She married and reared a family, not blaming God for lost opportunity, but asking him that some member of her family should one day go in her place.

When at last her son George surrendered to be a medical missionary—although he had not intended that sort of career and his mother had never made her call known to him— she was advanced in years. Because of her frailty, he hesitated to leave. "Son, I've prayed that God would not take me home," she told him finally, "until one of my children was on foreign soil as a missionary."

The sun was shining when George Leavell set foot on the coast of China. Back in Oxford, Mississippi, it was two o'clock in the morning when his mother died. Mrs. Leavell could have spent her years complaining that God had rejected her; but rather she prayed that God would multiply her. Those who know Baptist history will agree that the

Leavell family has probably contributed more Baptist leaders than any other family. We see proof that God was gracious to this faithful woman beyond all her dreams.

Future

All of us are interested in the future, both here and hereafter. Life is not a dead-end street for the Christian. Robert Browning, the famous English poet, expressed an optimistic view in *Rabbi Ben Ezra:*

> Grow old along with me! The best is yet to be,
> The last of life, for which the first was made.

That was what Paul was saying about his own life when he declared, "For to me to live is Christ, and to die is gain. . . . Nevertheless, to abide in the flesh is more needful for you" (Phil. 1:21-24).

One of our retired missionaries asked his doctor, after a physical examination, "How am I?"

"It looks like you are going to be with us for many years yet," the doctor replied.

"That's what I was afraid of!" the old warrior said. He was homesick for heaven; he knew that the best was yet to be.

The best that God has for his people is every hour that he gives them. In a former pastorate, I went with a young doctor to visit an elderly Sunday School teacher who was sick. We tried to tell her she ought to give up her class.

"Young man," she demanded of the doctor, "how old are most of your patients?" Then she explained, "I've lived longer than most of them. If I give up my class now, how long do you think I would last? I would rather just go on living with my Sunday School class." She did continue to live and serve for fifteen more years.

"Those that be planted in the house of the Lord," said the psalmist, "shall flourish in the courts of our God. They shall still bring forth fruit in old age" (92:13-14).

"What are you doing now?" a retired preacher was asked. "This year," he answered, "I am specializing in the study of Africa. I never had time for such things when I was pastoring." There is always so much to do, so much to build for, so much to learn!

We talk about ministry to youth, and the adolescent years as a very vital span; yet, they are only a brief part of life. There will come a time when, because of increasing longevity, we ought also to recognize a special ministry to the aged. The later years should be one of the happiest periods of life, when the battles are nearly over and the crown is almost in sight.

There is also a service needed *from* those who have lived longer. First, maintain a testimony that counts for Christ. "The steps of a good man are ordered by the Lord: and he delighteth in his way," you can affirm. "Though he fall, he shall not be utterly cast down: for the Lord upholdeth him with his hand. I have been young, and now am old; yet have I not seen the righteous forsaken, nor his seed begging bread" (Psalm 37:23-25).

The apostle Paul had something to say to older people about how they should conduct themselves: "That the aged men be sober, grave, temperate, sound in faith, in charity, in patience. The aged women likewise, that they be in behaviour as becometh holiness" (Titus 2:2-3). The older people should set the example.

A young mother, although pressed by duties, tries to send her children off to school with a prayer. But those who have a chance to sit quietly can spend more time in prayer. All of us need to become conscious of the great opportunity which these elderly saints of God have. Their prayers are a great untapped resource. If they can be helped to know that God hears their prayers for us, even though they are confined to their rooms, they could literally bring down victory upon every church.

Before a revival, one church called all of its shut-in members, asking them to pray during each service. Many of them responded with tearful voices, grateful that they were included. They must have prayed, because power came down for which there was no other explanation. "It was the first time I ever had to miss a revival," one of them said later, "but I don't guess I ever prayed more for my church in my life."

Young people need the counsel of experience, even though they frequently refuse to take it. If you have served God for many years, others need to know that you find him still the Good Shepherd. "The Lord will give grace and glory: no good thing will he withhold from them that walk uprightly" (Psalm 84:11).

You may not know how to make speeches, but a glowing, saintly life speaks eloquently for the Lord. Let your attendance be faithful as God grants you strength. Let his love show in your life. Demonstrate your faith and hope. Your ministry to the rest of us is needed. Teach us not to get so involved in other things that we miss that which is most important in the end—a life of fellowship with the Lord, in whom is all the security we need.

Beyond the Shadows

*Our Saviour Jesus Christ, who hath abolished
death, . . . hath brought life and immortality
to light through the gospel.* 2 Timothy 1:10

On the shelf of my library is a book written in 1881 by an
English minister. Its title, *Beyond the Shadows*, captured
my fancy, but inside is a most unusual dedication: "To the
Brotherhood of the Bereaved, to which I belong."

All of us, at some time, feel the heavy hand of death. We
speak of this great adventure beyond this vale of tears in
awesome tones. It is indeed a mystery; there are many
things about it which we do not and cannot know. But there
are some things about it which we ought to know with
positive assurance. If we remain ignorant, we sin against
ourselves and God, for he has revealed them on the pages
of his Word where we ought to search for them.

According to the Bible, beyond the shadows all is not unknown; it is sunrise rather than sunset. Thomas Hobbs, an
infidel, called "dying" a fearful leap into the dark. Another
wrote in poetic terms concerning death as "an experience
from which no traveler returns." Beautifully written, but
not true! The Lord Jesus Christ himself challenged such
statements. He did return after his death. For forty days he
appeared among men—on one occasion to five hundred people at once.

Before his death and resurrection, Jesus sat down with
his disciples one day and said to them, out of confident
knowledge, "Let not your heart be troubled: ye believe in

God, believe also in me. In my Father's house are many
mansions: if it were not so, I would have told you" (John
14:1-2). He promised that he would go and prepare a place
for his people so that we might be with him there.

Infidelity looks toward no bright future, and its adherents
have no songs. But we can sing because our

> Faith is built on nothing less
> Than Jesus' blood and righteousness.

Our loving Saviour would not leave us in a fog through
which we must find our way across a dread river Styx, nor
leave our path through the valley of the shadow unknown
and uncharted. Because he went before us, and returned,
we "won't have to cross Jordan alone."

There are many books being written today about death,
but the only valid answers are in the Bible. It matters little
what men's opinions concerning death may be, because they
have no firsthand knowledge. What Jesus has to say about
it makes all the difference in the world. "Can we know about
death?" the first-century Christians asked their great missionary, the apostle Paul. With assurance he declared, "This
we say unto you by the word of the Lord" (1 Thess. 4:15).
The reason some people fall into despair over death is that,
often, they know nothing about it.

Message of Death

It is astonishing that so many homes have no Bibles. There
are many families who never realize that they ought to have
a road map of life available. They spend their days as if
they thought they were going to stay here forever. Naturally, we want to stay as long as we can, but we shall not
stay forever. When the person without faith in God realizes
that fact, he searches restlessly for something—anything—

out beyond the limits of this life, but he usually looks in the wrong places.

Death is the world's most crowded freeway. It is the common experience of humanity, yet each man has to go through it alone, unless he is a Christian. All must die; thousands do every hour. No one can reasonably ignore the presence of death in human experience and the prevalence of decay in plant life. Observation of things about us indicates that we live in the land of the dying. But death is both a cessation and a beginning. It destroys our earthly bodies and transfers us to our eternal abode.

Yet, that death is the same "beautiful isle of somewhere" to everyone is foreign to the revealed Word of God. Many people think that the moment a man dies he becomes a saint, whether he lived like one or not. Where did they get such an idea? Certainly not from the Bible.

Some people say they have no fear about those who are lost, because they are "in the hands of a merciful God." But the Scriptures say that Jesus Christ, who has offered himself as the Saviour of mankind, will one day judge all the earth. Then what is the prospect for an individual who appears before the one he has rejected all his life? For the man who spurns the tremendous love of God in Christ, what is left but judgment with no room for mercy?

The Christian is promised "the resurrection of the just," but to the unsaved, the unbeliever, the Bible speaks in clear and positive terms of the "resurrection unto damnation." There is no better way to say it, no softer way, and maintain the truth before God.

The prospect of death has been simplified in the Negro spiritual, "goin' to lay down my burden, down by the riverside." But it is true that we will not have to worry about the burdens and sorrows of this life any longer. The things that Jesus said about death challenged the traditional ideas of those who heard him. Even in his earthly life, he experienced the opening of the heavens and the anointing of the Spirit. We see death only from our viewpoint in this present life, but Jesus had been on the other side.

Mankind thinks of death as a great darkness. It is true that this earthly sun is no longer visible to sightless eyes, but he who had experienced heaven firsthand said that it is bright over there with eternal light. Our sun sets here, but a new and brighter sun rises on that blissful shore.

We speak of death as a departure; heaven sees an arrival. We call death a hooded specter; heaven sees it as an angel of light. We call it separation; heaven calls it reunion. We call it a grave; heaven calls it a gateway. We say good-by here, but it is good morning up there. The sun sets here, but for the Christian, death is indeed sunrise with Jesus for eternity.

Mystery of Death

Love is often referred to as the "sweet mystery of life," but death has always been a dreaded mystery. To earthly eyes, it seems a silent, unsurveyed land.

You ask me what death is? I shall first have to ask you what life is, for death is not the same to all people. To the Christian, death is promotion; to the unbeliever, punishment. But to all it is a mystery.

It is certain that we shall die, but what takes place then is uncertain. None of us knows how he shall go, only that he will. Some say that when a man dies and his body decays, that is all. When the body is gone, the personality, being, and energy exist no more—annihilated, finished off as though one never existed in the first place.

Others say that while the body goes back into the earth,

the soul sleeps and knows nothing until Jesus knocks on
the grave and says, "Come forth." Then at the resurrection
the person arises as though he had been asleep only an hour
and is rested up to meet God and begin life anew. Still others say we exist in a disembodied state between dying in
our physical bodies and inhabiting the celestial bodies that
we shall have for eternity.

But what does the Bible say? By inference and example
the Bible teaches us that we shall know each other in heaven
—and also in hell. According to Jesus, the rich man in hell
opened his eyes, aware of the people there, conscious that
Lazarus was not there but in heaven. Names and relationships still existed, as did pain and hunger and thirst. The
man in hell did not dare plead his good works or the riches
he had possessed. His only basis for asking help was, "Back
on earth I knew Lazarus."

That is about as close to God as some people get. They
take out their religion in the name of a mother or a wife, a
friend, or a neighbor: "I had a godly father, a good mother,
or my friend so-and-so went to church. One of my uncles
was a preacher." But another man's religion is not enough.

Jesus said to the thief dying on the cross next to his, "To
day shalt thou be with me in paradise" (Luke 23:43). The
word carries the idea of a park, a celestial, perfect garden.
It is a beautiful idea, but the complete concept of never-
ending existence, of everlasting life, is beyond the grasp of
our finite minds. In a sense the Christian will truly experience life instead of death when he dies.

The Bible speaks of more than one heaven. First, the
heaven in which the birds fly—the atmosphere. Then there
is the heaven in which the stars shine—space as we know it.
"The third heaven," according to the apostle Paul, is where
God lives and where the spirits of our loved ones go to be

with him. This is the place of which Jesus was speaking when he promised, "Today thou shalt be with me in paradise."

Everyone has a lot of curiosity about death. Jesus' disciples asked him to tell them about it. The Pharisees and Sadducees and others tried to trick Jesus with questions about heaven and the after-life. "In the resurrection," they asked, "whose wife shall she be?"

"Ye do err," Jesus answered pointedly, "not knowing the scriptures, nor the power of God" (Matt. 22:28-29). "For he is not a God of the dead," Jesus added at another time, "but of the living: for all live unto him" (Luke 20:38).

The most sure and comforting word concerning the mystery of death was written by John, the beloved disciple. "Beloved, now are we the sons of God, and it doth not yet appear what we shall be: but we know that, when he shall appear, we shall be like him" (1 John 3:2). This is the comfort we can give each other, that we shall be like our Lord, that we shall have a resurrection body like his.

John was speaking of the appearances of Jesus as he came to his disciples between his resurrection and ascension. He had a body that was recognizable, one that had touchable flesh and bones, but yet was also glorified and powerful, able to go through locked doors and walk on the Emmaus road. That is really all we have to know.

Master of Death

Death is inescapable—it comes to everyone. Even the Son of God himself submitted to it, not because he could not escape, but to save mankind from its true horror, separation from God.

Death invades the castle as well as the cabin. No wall can be built high enough to keep death out. Somehow it is able to scale the highest mountain, leap the deepest sea. We cannot lock and bar the door but that death is able to open it and slip in. It is an experience that can come to a man regardless of where he is. It smothers out the lives of miners in the depths of the earth. It drowns out lives of sailors in the sea. It snuffs out lives of airmen in the heights of space. There is no place in the world or off it where death is not.

There is no place where we can get away from death or hide from the judgment of God. "If I ascend up into heaven, thou art there," said the psalmist. "If I make my bed in hell, behold, thou art there. If I take the wings of the morning, and dwell in the uttermost parts of the sea; even there shall thy hand lead me, and thy right hand shall hold me" (Psalm 139:8-10).

Then what hope do we have against the power of death and the certainty of judgment? We have no hope in ourselves, none at all. The sooner we realize that we live in dying, decaying bodies, alienated from God, the better off we are, because then we will come and say to the Great Physician, "Help me. Heal me. Make me whole."

Only Jesus can do that. The power of Jesus Christ can render death powerless forever. From Calvary's cross his body was taken and put into the tomb of his rich and silent disciple, Joseph of Arimathea, and his enemies sealed the tomb. Yet on the third day he arose again and declared to his disciples, "All power is given unto me in heaven and in earth" (Matt. 28:18).

It is true that our mortal bodies decay in the earth, but the Scriptures say that the angel of God shall come with a great trumpet to summon all the dead. God shall reach down into the bowels of the earth, his all-seeing eye shall search out the depths of the ocean, and he shall bring out every human body that has ever died from the beginning of time.

Not one soul, not one splinter of bone will be left in the grave or in the sea over which the devil might claim victory.

Then we will be able to chant with the apostle Paul and rejoice in the reality of victory. "O death, where is thy sting? O grave, where is thy victory? The sting of death is sin; and the strength of sin *is* the law. But thanks be to God, which giveth us the victory through our Lord Jesus Christ" (1 Cor. 15:55-57). Then we will be face to face with the Master of both life and death.

Death will terminate our earthly plans, our day of grace. There will not be another chance after death. Whatever decision you make, you must make in this life. A sign beside a gas station once read, "Free gas tomorrow." That was a safe promise, for tomorrow never comes. It always moves on ahead of us, just out of our reach.

Many people foolishly count on tomorrow. As the apostle James warned, "Whereas ye know not what shall be on the morrow. For what is your life? It is even a vapour, that appeareth for a little time, and then vanisheth away" (4:14). Life is always fleeting, and many times cut off very suddenly. "Behold, now is the accepted time; behold, now is the day of salvation" (2 Cor. 6:2).

However, for those who belong to God, his grace is unlimited and the future as bright as his love in Jesus Christ.

> O Hope of ev'ry contrite heart!
>   O Joy of all the meek!
> To those who fall, how kind thou art!
>   How good to those who seek!
>
> But what to those who find? ah, this,
>   No tongue or pen can show
> The love of Jesus, what it is
>   None but His loved ones know.

BERNARD OF CLAIRVAUX